Secret Diplomatic History of The Eighteenth Century

D1441551

Karl Marx

PUBLISHER'S PREFACE

In the Preface to "The Eastern Question," by Karl Marx, published in 1897, the Editors, Eleanor Marx Aveling and Edward Aveling, referred to two series of papers entitled "The Story of the Life of Lord Palmerston," and "Secret Diplomatic History of the Eighteenth Century," which they promised to publish at an early date.

Mrs. Aveling did not live long enough to see these papers through the press, but she left them in such a forward state, and we have had so many inquiries about them since, that we venture to issue them without Mrs. Aveling's final revision in two shilling pamphlets.

THE PUBLISHERS.

CONTENTS

CHAPTER I

No. 1. Mr. Rondeau to Horace Walpole.

"Petersburg, 17th August, 1736.

" ... I heartily wish ... that the Turks could be brought to condescend to make the first step, for this Court seems resolved to hearken to nothing till that is done, to mortify the Porte, that has on all occasions spoken of the Russians with the greatest contempt, which the Czarina and her present Ministers cannot bear. Instead of being obliged to Sir Everard Fawkner and Mr. Thalman (the former the British, the latter the Dutch Ambassador at Constantinople), for informing them of the good dispositions of the Turks, Count Oestermann will not be persuaded that the Porte is sincere, and seemed very much surprised that they had written to them (the Russian Cabinet) without order of the King and the States-General, or without being desired by the Grand Vizier, and that their letter had not been concerted with the Emperor's Minister at Constantinople.... I have shown Count Biron and Count Oestermann the two letters the Grand Vizier has written to the King, and at the same time told these gentlemen that as there was in them several hard reflections on this Court, I should not have communicated them if they had not been so desirous to see them. Count Biron said that was nothing, for they were used to be treated in this manner by the Turks. I desired their Excellencies not to let the Porte know that they had seen these letters, which would sooner aggravate matters than contribute to make them up...."

No. 2. Sir George Macartney to the Earl of Sandwich.

"St. Petersburg, 1st (12th) March, 1765.

"Most Secret.[2]

" ... Yesterday M. Panin[3] and the Vice-Chancellor, together with M. Osten, the Danish Minister, signed a treaty of alliance between this Court and that of Copenhagen. By one of the articles, a war with Turkey is made a casus fœderis; and whenever that event happens, Denmark binds herself to pay Russia a subsidy of 500,000 roubles per annum, by quarterly payments. Denmark also, by a most secret article, promises to disengage herself from all French connections, demanding only a limited time to endeavour to obtain the arrears due to her by the Court of France. At all events, she is immediately to enter into all the views of Russia in Sweden, and to act entirely, though not openly, with her in that kingdom. Either I am deceived or M. Gross[4] has misunderstood his instructions, when he told your lordship that Russia intended to stop short, and leave all the burden of Sweden upon England. However desirous this Court may be that we should pay a large proportion of every pecuniary engagement, yet, I am assured, she will always choose to take the lead at Stockholm. Her design, her ardent wish, is to make a common cause with England and Denmark, for the total annihilation of the French interest there. This certainly cannot be done without a considerable expense; but Russia, at present, does not seem unreasonable enough to expect that WE SHOULD PAY THE WHOLE. It has been hinted to me that £1,500 per annum, on our part, would be sufficient to support our interest, and absolutely prevent the French from ever getting at Stockholm again.

"The Swedes, highly sensible of, and very much mortified at, the dependent situation they have been in for many years, are extremely jealous of every Power that intermeddles in their affairs, and particularly so of their neighbours the Russians. This is the reason assigned to me for this Court's desiring that we and they should act upon SEPARATE bottoms, still preserving between our respective Ministers a confidence without reserve. That our first care should be, not to establish a faction under the name of a Russian or of an English faction; but, as even the wisest men are imposed upon by a mere name, to endeavour to have OUR friends distinguished as the friends of liberty and independence. At present we have a superiority, and the generality of the nation is persuaded how very ruinous their French connections have been, and, if continued, how very destructive they will be of their true interests. M. Panin does by no means desire that the smallest change should be made in the constitution of Sweden.[5] He wishes that the royal authority might be preserved without being augmented, and that the privileges of the people should be continued without violation. He was not, however, without his fears of the ambitious and intriguing spirit of the Queen, but the great ministerial vigilance of Count Oestermann has now entirely quieted his apprehensions on that head.

"By this new alliance with Denmark, and by the success in Sweden, which this Court has no doubt of, if properly seconded, M. Panin will, in some measure, have brought to bear his grand scheme of uniting the Powers of the North.[6] Nothing, then, will be wanted to render it entirely perfect, but the conclusion of a treaty alliance with Great Britain. I am persuaded this Court desires it most ardently. The Empress has expressed herself more than once, in terms that marked it strongly. Her ambition is to form, by such an union, a certain counterpoise to the family compact,[7] and to disappoint, as much as possible, all the views of the Courts of Vienna and Versailles, against which she is irritated with uncommon resentment. I am not, however, to conceal from your lordship that we can have no hope of any such alliance, unless we agree, by some secret article, to pay a subsidy in case of a Turkish war, for no money will be desired from us, except upon an emergency of that nature. I flatter myself I have persuaded this Court of the unreasonableness of expecting any subsidy in time of peace, and that an alliance upon an equal footing will be more safe and more honourable for both nations. I can assure your lordship that a Turkish war's being a casus fœderis, inserted either in the body of the treaty or in a secret article, will be a sine quâ non in every negotiation we may have to open with this Court. The obstinacy of M. Panin upon that point is owing to the accident I am going to mention. When the treaty between the Emperor and the King of Prussia was in agitation, the Count Bestoucheff, who is a mortal enemy to the latter, proposed the Turkish clause, persuaded that the King of Prussia would never submit to it, and flattering himself with the hopes of blowing up that negotiation by his refusal. But this old politician, it seemed, was mistaken in his conjecture, for his Majesty immediately consented to the proposal on condition that Russia should make no alliance with any other Power but on the same terms.[8] This is the real fact, and to confirm it, a few days since, Count Solme, the Prussian Minister, came to visit me, and told me that if this Court had any intention of concluding an alliance with ours without such a clause, he had orders to oppose it in the strongest manner. Hints have been given me that if Great Britain were less inflexible in that article, Russia will be less inflexible in the article of export duties in the Treaty of Commerce, which M. Gross told your lordship this Court would never depart from. I was assured at the same time, by a person in the highest degree of confidence with M. Panin, that if we entered upon the Treaty of Alliance the Treaty of Commerce would go on with it passibus æquis; that then the latter would be entirely taken out of the hands of the College of Trade, where so many cavils and altercations had been made, and would be settled only between the Minister and myself, and that he was sure it would be concluded to our satisfaction, provided the Turkish clause was admitted into the Treaty of Alliance. I was told, also, that in case the

Spaniards attacked Portugal, we might have 15,000 Russians in our pay to send upon that service. I must entreat your lordship on no account to mention to M. Gross the secret article of the Danish Treaty.... That gentleman, I am afraid, is no well-wisher to England."[9]

No. 3.—Sir James Harris to Lord Grantham.

"Petersburg, 16 (27 August), 1782.

"(Private.)

" ... On my arrival here I found the Court very different from what it had been described to me. So far from any partiality to England, its bearings were entirely French. The King of Prussia (then in possession of the Empress' ear) was exerting his influence against us. Count Panin assisted him powerfully; Lacy and Corberon, the Bourbon Ministers, were artful and intriguing; Prince Potemkin had been wrought upon by them; and the whole tribe which surrounded the Empress—the Schuwaloffs, Stroganoffs, and Chernicheffs—were what they still are, garçons perruquiers de Paris. Events seconded their endeavours. The assistance the French affected to afford Russia in settling its disputes with the Porte, and the two Courts being immediately after united as mediators at the Peace of Teschen, contributed not a little to reconcile them to each other. I was, therefore, not surprised that all my negotiations with Count Panin, from February, 1778, to July, 1779, should be unsuccessful, as he meant to prevent, not to promote, an alliance. It was in vain we made concessions to obtain it. He ever started fresh difficulties; had ever fresh obstacles ready. A very serious evil resulted, in the meanwhile, from my apparent confidence in him. He availed himself of it to convey in his reports to the Empress, not the language I employed, and the sentiments I actually expressed, but the language and sentiments he wished I should employ and express. He was equally careful to conceal her opinions and feelings from me; and while he described England to her as obstinate, and overbearing, and reserved, he described the Empress to me as displeased, disgusted, and indifferent to our concerns; and he was so convinced that, by this double misrepresentation, he had shut up every avenue of success that, at the time when I presented to him the Spanish declaration, he ventured to say to me, ministerially, 'That Great Britain had, by its own haughty conduct, brought down all its misfortunes on itself; that they were now at their height; that we must consent to any concession to obtain peace; and that we could expect neither assistance from our friends nor forbearance from our enemies.' I had temper enough not to give way to my feelings on this occasion.... I applied, without loss of time, to Prince Potemkin, and, by his means, the Empress condescended to see me alone at Peterhoff. I was so fortunate in this interview, as not only to efface all bad impressions she had against us, but by stating in its true light, our situation, and the inseparable interests of Great Britain and Russia, to raise in her mind a decided resolution to assist us. This resolution she declared to me in express words. When this transpired—and Count Panin was the first who knew it—he became my implacable and inveterate enemy. He not only thwarted by falsehoods and by a most undue exertion of his influence my public negotiations, but employed every means the lowest and most vindictive malice could suggest to depreciate and injure me personally; and from the very infamous accusations with which he charged me, had I been prone to fear, I might have apprehended the most infamous attacks at his hands. This relentless persecution still continues; it has outlived his Ministry. Notwithstanding the positive assurances I had received from the Empress herself, he found means, first to stagger, and afterwards to alter her resolutions. He was, indeed, very officiously assisted by his

3

Prussian Majesty, who, at the time, was as much bent on oversetting our interest as he now seems eager to restore it. I was not, however, disheartened by this first disappointment, and, by redoubling my efforts, I have twice more, during the course of my mission, brought the Empress to the verge (!) of standing forth our professed friend, and, each time, my expectations were grounded on assurances from her own mouth. The first was when our enemies conjured up the armed neutrality;[10] the other when Minorca was offered her. Although, on the first of these occasions, I found the same opposition from the same quarter I had experienced before, yet I am compelled to say that the principal cause of my failure was attributable to the very awkward manner in which we replied to the famous neutral declaration of February, 1780. As I well knew from what quarter the blow would come, I was prepared to parry it. My opinion was: 'If England feels itself strong enough to do without Russia, let it reject at once these new-fangled doctrines; but if its situation is such as to want assistance, let it yield to the necessity of the hour, recognise them as far as they relate to Russia alone, and by a well-timed act of complaisance insure itself a powerful friend.'[11] My opinion was not received; an ambiguous and trimming answer was given; we seemed equally afraid to accept or dismiss them. I was instructed secretly to oppose, but avowedly to acquiesce in them, and some unguarded expressions of one of its then confidential servants, made use of in speaking to Mr. Simolin, in direct contradiction to the temperate and cordial language that Minister had heard from Lord Stormont, irritated the Empress to the last degree, and completed the dislike and bad opinion she entertained of that Administration.[12] Our enemies took advantage of these circumstances.... I suggested the idea of giving up Minorca to the Empress, because, as it was evident to me we should at the peace be compelled to make sacrifices, it seemed to me wiser to make them to our friends than to our enemies. The idea was adopted at home in its whole extent,[13] and nothing could be more perfectly calculated to the meridian of this Court than the judicious instructions I received on this occasion from Lord Stormont. Why this project failed I am still at a loss to learn. I never knew the Empress incline so strongly to any one measure as she did to this, before I had my full powers to treat, nor was I ever more astonished than when I found her shrink from her purpose when they arrived. I imputed it at the same time, in my own mind, to the rooted aversion she had for our Ministry, and her total want of confidence in them; but I since am more strongly disposed to believe that she consulted the Emperor (of Austria) on the subject, and that he not only prevailed on her to decline the offer, but betrayed the secret to France, and that it thus became public. I cannot otherwise account for this rapid change of sentiment in the Empress, particularly as Prince Potemkin (whatever he might be in other transactions) was certainly in this cordial and sincere in his support, and both from what I saw at the time, and from what has since come to my knowledge, had its success at heart as much as myself. You will observe, my lord, that the idea of bringing the Empress forward as a friendly mediatrix went hand-in-hand with the proposed cession of Minorca. As this idea has given rise to what has since followed, and involved us in all the dilemmas of the present mediation, it will be necessary for me to explain what my views then were, and to exculpate myself from the blame of having placed my Court in so embarrassing a situation, my wish and intention was that she should be sole mediatrix without an adjoint; if you have perused what passed between her and me, in December, 1780, your lordship will readily perceive how very potent reasons I had to imagine she would be a friendly and even a partial one.[14] I knew, indeed, she was unequal to the task; but I knew, too, how greatly her vanity would be flattered by this distinction, and was well aware that when once engaged she would persist, and be inevitably involved in our quarrel, particularly when it should appear (and appear it would) that we had gratified her with Minorca. The annexing to the mediation the other (Austrian) Imperial Court entirely overthrew this plan. It not only afforded her a pretence for not keeping her word, but piqued and mortified her; and it was under this impression that she made over the whole business to the colleague we had given her, and ordered her Minister at Vienna to subscribe implicitly to whatever the Court proposed. Hence all the evils which have since arisen, and hence those we at this moment experience. I myself could never be brought to believe that the Court of Vienna, as long as Prince Kaunitz directs its measures, can mean England any good or France any harm. It was not with that view that I endeavoured to promote its influence here, but because I found that of Prussia in constant opposition to me; and because I thought that if I could by any means smite this, I should get rid of my greatest obstacle. I was mistaken, and, by a singular fatality, the Courts of Vienna and Berlin seem never to have agreed in anything but in the disposition to prejudice us here by turns.[15] The proposal relative to Minorca was the last attempt I made to induce the Empress to stand forth. I had exhausted my strength and resources; the freedom with which I had spoken in my last interview with her, though respectful, had displeased; and from this period to the removal of the late Administration, I have been reduced to act on the defensive.... I have had more difficulty in preventing the Empress from doing harm than I ever had in attempting to engage her to do us good. It was to prevent evil, that I inclined strongly for the acceptation of her single mediation between us and Holland, when her Imperial Majesty first offered it. The extreme dissatisfaction she expressed at our refusal justified my opinion; and I TOOK UPON ME, when it was proposed a second time, to urge the necessity of its being agreed to (ALTHOUGH I KNEW IT TO BE IN CONTRADICTION OF THE SENTIMENTS OF MY PRINCIPAL), since I firmly believed, had we again declined it, the Empress would, in a moment of anger, have joined the Dutch against us. As it is, all has gone on well; our judicious conduct has transferred to them the ill-humour she originally was in with us, and she now is as partial to our cause as she was before partial to theirs. Since the new Ministry in England, my road has been made smoother; the great and new path struck out by your predecessor,[16] and which you, my lord, pursue, has operated a most advantageous change in our favour upon the Continent. Nothing, indeed, but events which come home to her, will, I believe, ever induce her Imperial Majesty to take an active part; but there is now a strong glow of friendship in our favour; she approves our measures; she trusts our Ministry, and she gives way to that predilection she certainly has for our nation. Our enemies know and feel this; it keeps them in awe. This is a succinct but accurate sketch of what has passed at this Court from the day of my arrival at Petersburg to the present hour. Several inferences may be deduced from it.[17] That the Empress is led by her passions, not by reason and argument; that her prejudices are very strong, easily acquired, and, when once fixed, irremovable; while, on the contrary, there is no sure road to her good opinion; that even when obtained, it is subject to perpetual fluctuation, and liable to be biassed by the most trifling incidents; that till she is fairly embarked in a plan, no assurances can be depended on; but that when once fairly embarked, she never retracts, and may be carried any length; that with very bright parts, an elevated mind, an uncommon sagacity, she wants judgment, precision of idea, reflection, and L'ESPRIT DE COMBINAISON(!!) That her Ministers are either ignorant of, or indifferent to, the welfare of the State, and act from a passive submission to her will, or from motives of party and private interests."[18]

4. (Manuscript) Account of Russia during the commencement of the Reign of the Emperor Paul, drawn up by the Rev. L. K. Pitt, Chaplain to the Factory of St. Petersburg, and a near Relative of William Pitt.[19]

Extract.

"There can scarcely exist a doubt concerning the real sentiments of the late Empress of Russia on the great points which have, within the last few years, convulsed the whole system of

European politics. She certainly felt from the beginning the fatal tendency of the new principles, but was not, perhaps, displeased to see every European Power exhausting itself in a struggle which raised, in proportion to its violence, her own importance. It is more than probable that the state of the newly acquired provinces in Poland was likewise a point which had considerable influence over the political conduct of Catherine. The fatal effects resulting from an apprehension of revolt in the late seat of conquest seem to have been felt in a very great degree by the combined Powers, who in the early period of the Revolution were so near reinstating the regular Government in France. The same dread of revolt in Poland, which divided the attention of the combined Powers and hastened their retreat, deterred likewise the late Empress of Russia from entering on the great theatre of war, until a combination of circumstances rendered the progress of the French armies a more dangerous evil than any which could possibly result to the Russian Empire from active operations.... The last words which the Empress was known to utter were addressed to her Secretary when she dismissed him on the morning on which she was seized: 'Tell Prince' (Zuboff), she said, 'to come to me at twelve, and to remind me of signing the Treaty of Alliance with England.'"

Having entered into ample considerations on the Emperor Paul's acts and extravagances, the Rev. Mr. Pitt continues as follows:

"When these considerations are impressed on the mind, the nature of the late secession from the coalition, and of the incalculable indignities offered to the Government of Great Britain, can alone be fairly estimated.... But the ties which bind her (Great Britain) to the Russian Empire are formed by nature, and inviolable. United, these nations might almost brave the united world; divided, the strength and importance of each is FUNDAMENTALLY impaired. England has reason to regret with Russia that the imperial sceptre should be thus inconsistently wielded, but it is the sovereign of Russia alone who divides the Empires."

The reverend gentleman concludes his account by the words:

"As far as human foresight can at this moment penetrate, the despair of an enraged individual seems a more probable means to terminate the present scene of oppression than any more systematic combination of measures to restore the throne of Russia to its dignity and importance."

FOOTNOTES:

[1] This letter relates to the war against Turkey, commenced by the Empress Ann in 1735. The British diplomatist at St. Petersburg is reporting about his endeavours to induce Russia to conclude peace with the Turks. The passages omitted are irrelevant.

[2] England was at that time negotiating a commercial treaty with Russia.

[3] To this time it has remained among historians a point of controversy, whether or not Panin was in the pay of Frederick II. of Prussia, and whether he was so behind the back of Catherine, or at her bidding. There can exist no doubt that Catherine II., in order to identify foreign Courts with Russian Ministers, allowed Russian Ministers ostensibly to identify themselves with foreign Courts. As to Panin in particular, the question is, however, decided by an authentic document which we believe has never been published. It proves that, having once become the man of Frederick II., he was forced to remain so at the risk of his honour, fortune and life.

[4] The Russian Minister at London.

[5] The oligarchic Constitution set up by the Senate after the death of Charles XII.

[6] Thus we learn from Sir George Macartney that what is commonly known as Lord Chatham's "grand conception of the Northern Alliance," was, in fact, Panin's "grand scheme of uniting the Powers of the North." Chatham was duped into fathering the Muscovite plan.

[7] The compact between the Bourbons of France and Spain concluded at Paris on August, 1761.

[8] This was a subterfuge on the part of Frederick II. The manner in which Frederick was forced into the arms of the Russian Alliance is plainly told by M. Koch, the French professor of diplomacy and teacher of Talleyrand. "Frederick II.," he says, "having been abandoned by the Cabinet of London, could not but attach himself to Russia." (See his History of the Revolutions in Europe.)

[9] Horace Walpole characterises his epoch by the words—"It was the mode of the times to be paid by one favour for receiving another." At all events, it will be seen from the text that such was the mode of Russia in transacting business with England. The Earl of Sandwich, to whom Sir George Macartney could dare to address the above despatch, distinguished himself, ten years later, in 1775, as First Lord of the Admiralty, in the North Administration, by the vehement opposition he made to Lord Chatham's motion for an equitable adjustment of the American difficulties. "He could not believe it (Chatham's motion) the production of a British peer; it appeared to him rather the work of some American." In 1777, we find Sandwich again blustering: "he would hazard every drop of blood, as well as the last shilling of the national treasure, rather than allow Great Britain to be defied, bullied, and dictated to, by her disobedient and rebellious subjects." Foremost as the Earl of Sandwich was in entangling England in war with her North American colonies, with France, Spain, and Holland, we behold him constantly accused in Parliament by Fox, Burke, Pitt, etc., "of keeping the naval force inadequate to the defence of the country; of intentionally opposing small English forces where he knew the enemy to have concentrated large ones; of utter mismanagement of the service in all its departments," etc. (See debates of the House of Commons of 11th March, 1778; 31st March, 1778; February, 1779; Fox's motion of censure on Lord Sandwich; 9th April, 1779, address to the King for the dismissal of Lord Sandwich from his service, on account of misconduct in service; 7th February, 1782, Fox's motion that there had been gross mismanagement in the administration of naval affairs during the year 1781.) On this occasion Pitt imputed to Lord Sandwich "all our naval disasters and disgraces." The ministerial majority against the motion amounted to only 22 in a House of 388. On the 22nd February, 1782, a similar motion against Lord Sandwich was only negatived by a majority of 19 in a House of 453. Such, indeed, was the character of the Earl of Sandwich's Administration that more than thirty distinguished officers quitted the naval service, or declared they could not act under the existing system. In point of fact, during his whole tenure of office, serious apprehensions were entertained of the consequences of the dissensions then prevalent in the navy. Besides, the Earl of Sandwich was openly accused, and, as far as circumstantial evidence goes, convicted of Peculation. (See debates of the House of Lords, 31st March, 1778; 9th April, 1779, and seq.) When the motion for his removal from office was negatived on April 9th 1779, thirty-nine peers entered their protest.

[10] Sir James Harris affects to believe that Catherine II. was not the author of, but a convert to, the armed neutrality of 1780. It is one of the grand stratagems of the Court of St. Petersburg to give to its own schemes the form of proposals suggested to and pressed on itself by foreign Courts. Russian diplomacy delights in those quæ pro quo. Thus the Court of

Florida Bianca was made the responsible editor of the armed neutrality, and, from a report that vain-glorious Spaniard addressed to Carlos III., one may see how immensely he felt flattered at the idea of having not only hatched the armed neutrality but allured Russia into abetting it.

[11] This same Sir James Harris, perhaps more familiar to the reader under the name of the Earl of Malmesbury, is extolled by English historians as the man who prevented England from surrendering the right of search in the Peace Negotiations of 1782-83.

[12] It might be inferred from this passage and similar ones occurring in the text, that Catherine II. had caught a real Tartar in Lord North, whose Administration Sir James Harris is pointing at. Any such delusion will disappear before the simple statement that the first partition of Poland took place under Lord North's Administration, without any protest on his part. In 1773 Catherine's war against Turkey still continuing, and her conflicts with Sweden growing serious, France made preparations to send a powerful fleet into the Baltic. D'Aiguillon, the French Minister of Foreign Affairs, communicated this plan to Lord Stormont, the then English Ambassador at Paris. In a long conversation, D'Aiguillon dwelt largely on the ambitious designs of Russia, and the common interest that ought to blend France and England into a joint resistance against them. In answer to this confidential communication, he was informed by the English Ambassador that, "if France sent her ships into the Baltic, they would instantly be followed by a British fleet; that the presence of two fleets would have no more effect than a neutrality; and however the British Court might desire to preserve the harmony now subsisting between England and France, it was impossible to foresee the contingencies that might arise from accidental collision." In consequence of these representations, D'Aiguillon countermanded the squadron at Brest, but gave new orders for the equipment of an armament at Toulon. "On receiving intelligence of these renewed preparations, the British Cabinet made instant and vigorous demonstrations of resistance; Lord Stormont was ordered to declare that every argument used respecting the Baltic applied equally to the Mediterranean. A memorial also was presented to the French Minister, accompanied by a demand that it should be laid before the King and Council. This produced the desired effect; the armament was countermanded, the sailors disbanded, and the chances of an extensive warfare avoided."

"Lord North," says the complacent writer from whom we have borrowed the last lines, "thus effectually served the cause of his ally (Catherine II.), and facilitated the treaty of peace (of Kutchuk-Kainardji) between Russia and the Porte." Catherine II. rewarded Lord North's good services, first by withholding the aid she had promised him in case of a war between England and the North American Colonies, and in the second place, by conjuring up and leading the armed neutrality against England. Lord North DARED NOT repay, as he was advised by Sir James Harris, this treacherous breach of faith by giving up to Russia, and to Russia alone, the maritime rights of Great Britain. Hence the irritation in the nervous system of the Czarina; the hysterical fancy she caught all at once of "entertaining a bad opinion" of Lord North, of "disliking" him, of feeling a "rooted aversion" against him, of being afflicted with "a total want of confidence," etc. In order to give the Shelburne Administration a warning example, Sir James Harris draws up a minute psychological picture of the feelings of the Czarina, and the disgrace incurred by the North Administration, for having wounded these same feelings. His prescription is very simple: surrender to Russia, as our friend, everything for asking which we would consider every other Power our enemy.

[13] It is then a fact that the English Government, not satisfied with having made Russia a Baltic power, strove hard to make her a Mediterranean power too. The offer of the surrender of Minorca appears to have been made to Catherine II. at the end of 1779, or the beginning

of 1780, shortly after Lord Stormont's entrance into the North Cabinet—the same Lord Stormont we have seen thwarting the French attempts at resistance against Russia, and whom even Sir James Harris cannot deny the merit of having written "instructions perfectly calculated to the meridian of the Court of St. Petersburg." While Lord North's Cabinet, at the suggestion of Sir James Harris, offered Minorca to the Muscovites, the English Commoners and people were still trembling for fear lest the Hanoverians (?) should wrest out of their hands "one of the keys of the Mediterranean." On the 26th of October, 1775, the King, in his opening speech, had informed Parliament, amongst other things, that he had Sir James Graham's own words, when asked why they should not have kept up some blockade pending the settlement of the "plan," "They did not take that responsibility upon themselves." The responsibility of executing their orders! The despatch we have quoted is the only despatch read, except one of a later date. The despatch, said to be sent on the 5th of April, in which "the Admiral is ordered to use the largest discretionary power in blockading the Russian ports in the Black Sea," is not read, nor any replies from Admiral Dundas. The Admiralty sent Hanoverian troops to Gibraltar and Port Mahon (Minorca), to replace such British regiments as should be drawn from those garrisons for service in America. An amendment to the address was proposed by Lord John Cavendish, strongly condemning "the confiding such important fortresses as Gibraltar and Port Mahon to foreigners." After very stormy debates, in which the measure of entrusting Gibraltar and Minorca, "the keys of the Mediterranean," as they were called, to foreigners, was furiously attacked; Lord North, acknowledging himself the adviser of the measure, felt obliged to bring in a bill of indemnity. However, these foreigners, these Hanoverians, were the English King's own subjects. Having virtually surrendered Minorca to Russia in 1780, Lord North was, of course, quite justified in treating, on November 22, 1781, in the House of Commons, "with utter scorn the insinuation that Ministers were in the pay of France."

Let us remark, en passant, that Lord North, one of the most base and mischievous Ministers England can boast of, perfectly mastered the art of keeping the House in perpetual laughter. So had Lord Sunderland. So has Lord Palmerston.

[14] Lord North having been supplanted by the Rockingham Administration, on March 27, 1782, the celebrated Fox forwarded peace proposals to Holland through the mediation of the Russian Minister. Now what were the consequences of the Russian mediation so much vaunted by this Sir James Harris, the servile account keeper of the Czarina's sentiments, humours, and feelings? While preliminary articles of peace had been convened with France, Spain, and the American States, it was found impossible to arrive at any such preliminary agreement with Holland. Nothing but a simple cessation of hostilities was to be obtained from it. So powerful proved the Russian mediation, that on the 2nd September, 1783, just one day before the conclusion of definitive treaties with America, France, and Spain, Holland condescended to accede to preliminaries of peace, and this not in consequence of the Russian mediation, but through the influence of France.

[15] How much was England not prejudiced by the Courts of Vienna and Paris thwarting the plan of the British Cabinet of ceding Minorca to Russia, and by Frederick of Prussia's resistance against the great Chatham's scheme of a Northern Alliance under Muscovite auspices.

[16] The predecessor is Fox. Sir James Harris establishes a complete scale of British Administrations, according to the degree in which they enjoyed the favour of his almighty Czarina. In spite of Lord Stormont, the Earl of Sandwich, Lord North, and Sir James Harris himself; in spite of the partition of Poland, the bullying of D'Aiguillon, the treaty of Kutchuk-Kainardji, and the intended cession of Minorca—Lord North's Administration is relegated

to the bottom of the heavenly ladder; far above it has climbed the Rockingham Administration, whose soul was Fox, notorious for his subsequent intrigues with Catherine; but at the top we behold the Shelburne Administration, whose Chancellor of the Exchequer was the celebrated William Pitt. As to Lord Shelburne himself, Burke exclaimed in the House of Commons, that "if he was not a Catalina or Borgia in morals, it must not be ascribed to anything but his understanding."

[17] Sir James Harris forgets deducing the main inference, that the Ambassador of England is the agent of Russia.

[18] In the 18th century, English diplomatists' despatches, bearing on their front the sacramental inscription, "Private," are despatches to be withheld from the King by the Minister to whom they are addressed. That such was the case may be seen from Lord Mahon's History of England.

[19] "To be burnt after my death." Such are the words prefixed to the manuscript by the gentleman whom it was addressed to.

CHAPTER II

The documents published in the first chapter extend from the reign of the Empress Ann to the commencement of the reign of the Emperor Paul, thus encompassing the greater part of the 18th century. At the end of that century it had become, as stated by the Rev. Mr. Pitt, the openly professed and orthodox dogma of English diplomacy, "that the ties which bind Great Britain to the Russian Empire are formed by nature, and inviolable."

In perusing these documents, there is something that startles us even more than their contents—viz., their form. All these letters are "confidential," "private," "secret," "most secret"; but in spite of secrecy, privacy, and confidence, the English statesmen converse among each other about Russia and her rulers in a tone of awful reserve, abject servility, and cynical submission, which would strike us even in the public despatches of Russian statesmen. To conceal intrigues against foreign nations secrecy is recurred to by Russian diplomatists. The same method is adopted by English diplomatists freely to express their devotion to a foreign Court. The secret despatches of Russian diplomatists are fumigated with some equivocal perfume. It is one part the fumée de fausseté, as the Duke of St. Simon has it, and the other part that coquettish display of one's own superiority and cunning which stamps upon the reports of the French Secret Police their indelible character. Even the master despatches of Pozzo di Borgo are tainted with this common blot of the littérature de mauvais lieu. In this point the English secret despatches prove much superior. They do not affect superiority but silliness. For instance, can there be anything more silly than Mr. Rondeau informing Horace Walpole that he has betrayed to the Russian Minister the letters addressed by the Turkish Grand Vizier to the King of England, but that he had told "at the same time those gentlemen that as there were several hard reflections on the Russian Court he should not have communicated them, if they had not been so anxious to see them," and then told their excellencies not to tell the Porte that they had seen them (those letters)! At first view the infamy of the act is drowned in the silliness of the man. Or, take Sir George Macartney. Can there be anything more silly than his happiness that Russia seemed "reasonable" enough not to expect that England "should pay the WHOLE EXPENSES" for Russia's "choosing to take the lead at Stockholm"; or his "flattering himself" that he had "persuaded the Russian Court" not to be so "unreasonable" as to ask from England, in a time of peace, subsidies for a time of war against Turkey (then the ally of England); or his warning the Earl of Sandwich "not to mention" to the Russian Ambassador at London the secrets mentioned to himself by the Russian Chancellor at St. Petersburg? Or can there be anything more silly than Sir James Harris confidentially whispering into the ear of Lord Grantham that Catherine II. was devoid of "judgment, precision of idea, reflection, and l'esprit de combinaison"?[20]

On the other hand, take the cool impudence with which Sir George Macartney informs his minister that because the Swedes were extremely jealous of, and mortified at, their dependence on Russia, England was directed by the Court of St. Petersburg to do its work at Stockholm, under the British colours of liberty and independence! Or Sir James Harris advising England to surrender to Russia Minorca and the right of search, and the monopoly of mediation in the affairs of the world—not in order to gain any material advantage, or even a formal engagement on the part of Russia, but only "a strong glow of friendship" from the Empress, and the transfer to France of her "ill humour."

The secret Russian despatches proceed on the very plain line that Russia knows herself to have no common interests whatever with other nations, but that every nation must be persuaded separately to have common interests with Russia to the exclusion of every other nation. The English despatches, on the contrary, never dare so much as hint that Russia has common interests with England, but only endeavour to convince England that she has Russian interests. The English diplomatists themselves tell us that this was the single argument they pleaded, when placed face to face with Russian potentates.

If the English despatches we have laid before the public were addressed to private friends, they would only brand with infamy the ambassadors who wrote them. Secretly addressed as they are to the British Government itself, they nail it for ever to the pillory of history; and, instinctively, this seems to have been felt, even by Whig writers, because none has dared to publish them.

The question naturally arises from which epoch this Russian character of English diplomacy, become traditionary in the course of the 18th century, does date its origin. To clear up this point we must go back to the time of Peter the Great, which, consequently, will form the principal subject of our researches. We propose to enter upon this task by reprinting some English pamphlets, written at the time of Peter I., and which have either escaped the attention of modern historians, or appeared to them to merit none. However, they will suffice for refuting the prejudice common to Continental and English writers, that the designs of Russia were not understood or suspected in England until at a later, and too late, epoch; that the diplomatic relations between England and Russia were but the natural offspring of the mutual material interests of the two countries; and that, therefore, in accusing the British statesmen of the 18th century of Russianism we should commit an unpardonable hysteron-proteron. If we have shown by the English despatches that, at the time of the Empress Ann, England already betrayed her own allies to Russia, it will be seen from the pamphlets we are now about to reprint that, even before the epoch of Ann, at the very epoch of Russian ascendency in Europe, springing up at the time of Peter I., the plans of Russia were understood, and the connivance of British statesmen at these plans was denounced by English writers.

The first pamphlet we lay before the public is called The Northern Crisis. It was printed in London in 1716, and relates to the intended Dano-Anglo-Russian invasion of Skana (Schonen).

During the year 1715 a northern alliance for the partition, not of Sweden proper, but of what we may call the Swedish Empire, had been concluded between Russia, Denmark, Poland, Prussia, and Hanover. That partition forms the first grand act of modern diplomacy—the logical premiss to the partition of Poland. The partition treaties relating to Spain have engrossed the interest of posterity because they were the forerunners of the War of Succession, and the partition of Poland drew even a larger audience because its last act was played upon a contemporary stage. However, it cannot be denied that it was the partition of the Swedish Empire which inaugurated the modern era of international policy. The partition treaty not even pretended to have a pretext, save the misfortune of its intended victim. For the first time in Europe the violation of all treaties was not only made, but proclaimed the common basis of a new treaty. Poland herself, in the drag of Russia, and personated by that commonplace of immorality, Augustus II., Elector of Saxony and King of Poland, was pushed into the foreground of the conspiracy, thus signing her own death-warrant, and not even enjoying the privilege reserved by Polyphemus to Odysseus—to be last eaten. Charles XII. predicted her fate in the manifesto flung against King Augustus and the Czar, from his voluntary exile at Bender. The manifesto is dated January 28, 1711.

The participation in this partition treaty threw England within the orbit of Russia, towards whom, since the days of the "Glorious Revolution," she had more and more gravitated. George I., as King of England, was bound to a defensive alliance with Sweden by the treaty of 1700. Not only as King of England, but as Elector of Hanover, he was one of the guarantees, and even of the direct parties to the treaty of Travendal, which secured to Sweden what the partition treaty intended stripping her of. Even his German electoral dignity he partly owed to that treaty. However, as Elector of Hanover he declared war against Sweden, which he waged as King of England.

In 1715 the confederates had divested Sweden of her German provinces, and to effect that end introduced the Muscovite on the German soil. In 1716 they agreed to invade Sweden Proper—to attempt an armed descent upon Schonen—the southern extremity of Sweden now constituting the districts of Malmoe and Christianstadt. Consequently Peter of Russia brought with him from Germany a Muscovite army, which was scattered over Zealand, thence to be conveyed to Schonen, under the protection of the English and Dutch fleets sent into the Baltic, on the false pretext of protecting trade and navigation. Already in 1715, when Charles XII. was besieged in Stralsund, eight English men-of-war, lent by England to Hanover, and by Hanover to Denmark, had openly reinforced the Danish navy, and even hoisted the Danish flag. In 1716 the British navy was commanded by his Czarish Majesty in person.

Everything being ready for the invasion of Schonen, there arose a difficulty from a side where it was least expected. Although the treaty stipulated only for 30,000 Muscovites, Peter, in his magnanimity, had landed 40,000 on Zealand; but now that he was to send them on the errand to Schonen, he all at once discovered that out of the 40,000 he could spare but 15,000. This declaration not only paralysed the military plan of the confederates, it seemed to threaten the security of Denmark and of Frederick IV., its king, as great part of the Muscovite army, supported by the Russian fleet, occupied Copenhagen. One of the generals of Frederick proposed suddenly to fall with the Danish cavalry upon the Muscovites and to exterminate them, while the English men-of-war should burn the Russian fleet. Averse to any perfidy which required some greatness of will, some force of character, and some contempt of personal danger, Frederick IV. rejected the bold proposal, and limited himself to assuming an attitude of defence. He then wrote a begging letter to the Czar, intimating that he had given up his Schonen fancy, and requested the Czar to do the same and find his way home: a request the latter could not but comply with. When Peter at last left Denmark with his army,

12

the Danish Court thought fit to communicate to the Courts of Europe a public account of the incidents and transactions which had frustrated the intended descent upon Schonen— and this document forms the starting point of The Northern Crisis.

In a letter addressed to Baron Görtz, dated from London, January 23, 1717, by Count Gyllenborg, there occur some passages in which the latter, the then Swedish ambassador at the Court of St. James's, seems to profess himself the author of The Northern Crisis, the title of which he does not, however, quote. Yet any idea of his having written that powerful pamphlet will disappear before the slightest perusal of the Count's authenticated writings, such as his letters to Görtz.

"The Northern Crisis; or Impartial Reflections on the Policies of the Czar; occasioned by Mynheer Von Stocken's Reasons for delaying the descent upon Schonen. A true copy of which is prefixed, verbally translated after the tenor of that in the German Secretary's Office in Copenhagen, October 10, 1716. London, 1716.

1.—Preface——— ... 'Tis (the present pamphlet) not fit for lawyers' clerks, but it is highly convenient to be read by those who are proper students in the laws of nations; 'twill be but lost time for any stock-jobbing, trifling dealer in Exchange-Alley to look beyond the preface on't, but every merchant in England (more especially those who trade to the Baltic) will find his account in it. The Dutch (as the courants and postboys have more than once told us) are about to mend their hands, if they can, in several articles of trade with the Czar, and they have been a long time about it to little purpose. Inasmuch as they are such a frugal people, they are good examples for the imitation of our traders; but if we can outdo them for once, in the means of projecting a better and more expeditious footing to go upon, for the emolument of us both, let us, for once, be wise enough to set the example, and let them, for once, be our imitators. This little treatise will show a pretty plain way how we may do it, as to our trade in the Baltic, at this juncture. I desire no little coffee-house politician to meddle with it; but to give him even a disrelish for my company. I must let him know that he is not fit for mine. Those who are even proficients in state science, will find in it matter highly fit to employ all their powers of speculation, which they ever before past negligently by, and thought (too cursorily) were not worth the regarding. No outrageous party-man will find it at all for his purpose; but every honest Whig and every honest Tory may each of them read it, not only without either of their disgusts, but with the satisfaction of them both.... 'Tis not fit, in fine, for a mad, hectoring, Presbyterian Whig, or a raving, fretful, dissatisfied, Jacobite Tory."

2.—The reasons handed about by Mynheer Von Stocken for delaying the descent upon Schonen.

"There being no doubt, but most courts will be surprised that the descent upon Schonen has not been put into execution, notwithstanding the great preparations made for that purpose; and that all his Czarish Majesty's troops, who were in Germany, were transported to Zealand, not without great trouble and danger, partly by his own gallies, and partly by his Danish Majesty's and other vessels; and that the said descent is deferred till another time. His Danish Majesty hath therefore, in order to clear himself of all imputation and reproach, thought fit to order, that the following true account of this affair should be given to all impartial persons. Since the Swedes were entirely driven out of their German dominions, there was, according to all the rules of policy, and reasons of war, no other way left, than vigorously to attack the still obstinate King of Sweden, in the very heart of his country; thereby, with God's assistance, to force him to a lasting, good and advantageous peace for the allies. The King of Denmark and his Czarish Majesty were both of this opinion, and did, in order to put so good a design in execution, agree upon an interview, which at last (notwithstanding his Danish Majesty's presence, upon the account of Norway's being invaded, was most necessary in his own capital, and that the Muscovite ambassador, M. Dolgorouky, had given quite other assurances) was held at Ham and Horn, near Hamburgh, after his Danish Majesty had stayed there six weeks for the Czar. In this conference it was, on the 3rd of June, agreed between both their Majesties, after several debates, that the descent upon Schonen should positively be undertaken this year, and everything relating to the forwarding the same was entirely consented to. Hereupon his Danish Majesty made all haste for his return to his dominions, and gave orders to work day and night to get his fleet ready to put to sea. The transport ships were also gathered from all parts of his dominions, both with inexpressible charges and great prejudice to his subjects' trade. Thus, his Majesty (as the Czar himself upon his arrival at Copenhagen owned) did his utmost to provide all necessaries, and to forward the descent, upon whose success everything depended. It happened, however, in the meanwhile, and before the descent was agreed upon in the conference at Ham and Horn, that his Danish Majesty was obliged to secure his invaded and much oppressed kingdom of Norway, by sending thither a considerable squadron out of his fleet, under the command of Vice-Admiral Gabel, which squadron could not be recalled before the enemy had left that kingdom, without endangering a great part thereof; so that out of necessity the said Vice-Admiral was forced to tarry there till the 12th of July, when his Danish Majesty sent him express orders to return with all possible speed, wind and weather permitting; but this blowing for some time contrary, he was detained.... The Swedes were all the while powerful at sea, and his Czarish Majesty himself did not think it advisable that the remainder of the Danish, in conjunction with the men-of-war then at Copenhagen, should go to convoy the Russian troops from Rostock, before the above-mentioned squadron under Vice-Admiral Gabel was arrived. This happening at last in the month of August, the confederate fleet put to sea; and the transporting of the said troops hither to Zealand was put in execution, though with a great deal of trouble and danger, but it took up so much time that the descent could not be ready till September following. Now, when all these preparations, as well for the descent as the embarking the armies, were entirely ready, his Danish Majesty assured himself that the descent should be made within a few days, at farthest by the 21st of September. The Russian Generals and Ministers first raised some difficulties to those of Denmark, and afterwards, on the 17th September, declared in an appointed conference, that his Czarish Majesty, considering the present situation of affairs, was of opinion that neither forage nor provision could be had in Schonen, and that consequently the descent was not advisable to be attempted this year, but ought to be put off till next spring. It may easily be imagined how much his Danish Majesty was surprised at this; especially seeing the Czar, if he had altered his opinion, as to this design so solemnly concerted, might have declared it sooner, and thereby saved his Danish Majesty several tons of gold, spent upon the necessary preparations. His Danish Majesty did, however, in a letter dated the 20th of September, amply represent to the Czar, that although the season was very much advanced, the descent might, nevertheless, easily be undertaken with such a superior force, as to get a footing in Schonen, where being assured there had been a very plentiful harvest, he did not doubt but subsistence might be found; besides, that having an open communication with his own countries, it might easily be transported from thence. His Danish Majesty alleged also several weighty reasons why the descent was either to be made this year, or the thoughts of making it next spring entirely be laid aside. Nor did he alone make these moving remonstrances to the Czar; but his British Majesty's Minister residing here, as well as Admiral Norris, seconded the same also in a very pressing manner; and by express order of the King, their master, endeavoured to bring the Czar into their opinion, and to persuade him to go on with the descent; but his Czarish Majesty declared by his answer, that he would adhere to the resolution that he had once taken concerning this delay of making the descent; but if his Danish Majesty was resolved to venture on the descent, that he then, according to the treaty made near Straelsund, would assist him only with the 15 battalions and 1,000 horse therein stipulated; that next spring he would comply with everything else, and neither could or would declare himself farther in this affair. Since then, his Danish Majesty could not, without running so great a hazard, undertake so great a work alone with his own army and the said 15 battalions; he desired, in another letter of the 23rd September, his Czarish Majesty would be pleased to add 13 battalions of his troops, in which case his Danish Majesty would still this year attempt the descent; but even this could not be obtained from his Czarish Majesty, who absolutely refused it by his ambassador on the 24th ditto: whereupon his Danish Majesty, in his letter of the 26th, declared to the Czar, that since things stood thus, he desired none of his troops, but that they might be all speedily transported out of his dominions; that so the transport, whose freight stood him in 40,000 rix dollars per month, might be discharged, and his subjects eased of the intolerable contributions they now underwent. This he could not do less than agree to; and accordingly, all the Russian troops are already embarked, and intend for certain to go from here with the first favourable wind. It must be left to Providence and time, to discover what may have induced the Czar to a resolution so prejudicial to the Northern Alliance, and most advantageous to the common enemy.

If we would take a true survey of men, and lay them open in a proper light to the eye of our intellects, we must first consider their natures and then their ends; and by this method of examination, though their conduct is, seemingly, full of intricate mazes and perplexities, and winding round with infinite meanders of state-craft, we shall be able to dive into the deepest recesses, make our way through the most puzzling labyrinths, and at length come to the most abstruse means of bringing about the master secrets of their minds, and to unriddle their utmost mysteries.... The Czar ... is, by nature, of a great and enterprising spirit, and of a genius thoroughly politic; and as for his ends, the manner of his own Government, where he sways arbitrary lord over the estates and honours of his people, must make him, if all the policies in the world could by far-distant aims promise him accession and accumulation of empire and wealth, be everlastingly laying schemes for the achieving of both with the extremest cupidity and ambition. Whatever ends an insatiate desire of opulency, and a boundless thirst for dominion, can ever put him upon, to satisfy their craving and voracious appetites, those must, most undoubtedly, be his.

The next questions we are to put to ourselves are these three:

1. By what means can he gain these ends?

2. How far from him, and in what place, can these ends be best obtained?

3. And by what time, using all proper methods and succeeding in them, may he obtain these ends?

The possessions of the Czar were prodigious, vast in extent; the people all at his nod, all his downright arrant slaves, and all the wealth of the country his own at a word's command. But then the country, though large in ground, was not quite so in produce. Every vassal had his gun, and was to be a soldier upon call; but there was never a soldier among them, nor a man that understood the calling; and though he had all their wealth, they had no commerce of consequence, and little ready money; and consequently his treasury, when he had amassed all he could, very bare and empty. He was then but in an indifferent condition to satisfy those two natural appetites, when he had neither wealth to support a soldiery, nor a soldiery trained in the art of war. The first token this Prince gave of an aspiring genius, and of an ambition that is noble and necessary in a monarch who has a mind to flourish, was to believe none of his subjects more wise than himself, or more fit to govern. He did so, and looked upon his own proper person as the most fit to travel out among the other realms of the world and study politics for the advancing of his dominions. He then seldom pretended to any warlike dispositions against those who were instructed in the science of arms; his military dealings lay mostly with the Turks and Tartars, who, as they had numbers as well as he, had them likewise composed, as well as his, of a rude, uncultivated mob, and they appeared in the field like a raw, undisciplined militia. In this his Christian neighbours liked him well, insomuch as he was a kind of stay or stopgap to the infidels. But when he came to look into the more polished parts of the Christian world, he set out towards it, from the very threshold, like a natural-born politician. He was not for learning the game by trying chances and venturing losses in the field so soon; no, he went upon the maxim that it was, at that time of day, expedient and necessary for him to carry, like Samson, his strength in his head, and not in his arms. He had then, he knew, but very few commodious places for commerce of his own, and those all situated in the White Sea, too remote, frozen up the most part of the year, and not at all fit for a fleet of men-of-war; but he knew of many more commodious ones of his neighbours in the Baltic, and within his reach whenever he could strengthen his hands to lay hold of them. He had a longing eye towards them; but with prudence seemingly turned his head another way, and secretly entertained the pleasant thought that he should come at them all in good time. Not to give any jealousy, he endeavours for no help from his neighbours to instruct his men in arms. That was like asking a skilful person, one intended to fight a duel with, to teach him first how to fence. He went over to Great Britain, where he knew that potent kingdom could, as yet, have no jealousies of his growth of power, and in the eye of which his vast extent of nation lay neglected and unconsidered and overlooked, as I am afraid it is to this very day. He was present at all our exercises, looked into all our laws, inspected our military, civil, and ecclesiastical regimen of affairs; yet this was the least he then wanted; this was the slightest part of his errand. But by degrees, when he grew familiar with our people, he visited our docks, pretending not to have any prospect of profit, but only to take a huge delight (the effect of curiosity only) to see our manner of building ships. He kept his court, as one may say, in our shipyard, so industrious was he in affording them his continual Czarish presence, and to his immortal glory for art and industry be it spoken, that the great Czar, by stooping often to the employ, could handle an axe with the best artificer of them all; and the monarch having a good mathematical head of his own, grew in some time a very expert royal shipwright. A ship or two for his diversion made and sent him, and then two or three more, and after that two or three more, would signify just nothing at all, if they were granted to be sold to him by the Maritime Powers, that could, at will, lord it over the sea. It would be a puny inconsiderable matter, and not worth the regarding. Well, but then, over and above this, he had artfully insinuated himself into the goodwill of many of our best workmen, and won their hearts by his good-natured familiarities and condescension among them. To turn this to his service, he offered many very large premiums and advantages to go and settle in his country, which they gladly accepted of. A little after he sends over some private ministers and officers to negotiate for more workmen, for land officers, and likewise for picked and chosen good seamen, who might be advanced and promoted to offices by going there. Nay, even to this day, any expert seaman that is upon our traffic to the port of Archangel, if he has the least spark of ambition and any ardent desire to be in office, he need but offer himself to the sea-service of the Czar, and he is a lieutenant immediately. Over and above this, that Prince has even found the way to take by force into his service out of our merchant ships as many of their ablest seamen as he pleased, giving the masters the same number of raw Muscovites in their place, whom they afterwards were forced in their own defence to make fit for their own use. Neither is this all; he had, during the last war, many hundreds of his subjects, both noblemen and common sailors, on board ours, the French and the Dutch fleets; and he has all along maintained, and still maintains numbers of them in ours and the Dutch yards.

But seeing he looked all along upon all these endeavours towards improving himself and his subjects as superfluous, whilst a seaport was wanting, where he might build a fleet of his own, and from whence he might himself export the products of his country, and import those of others; and finding the King of Sweden possessed of the most convenient ones, I mean Narva and Revel, which he knew that Prince never could nor would amicably part with, he at last resolved to wrest them out of his hands by force. His Swedish Majesty's tender youth seemed the fittest time for this enterprise, but even then he would not run the hazard alone. He drew in other princes to divide the spoil with him. And the Kings of Denmark and Poland were weak enough to serve as instruments to forward the great and ambitious views of the Czar. It is true, he met with a mighty hard rub at his very first setting out; his whole army being entirely defeated by a handful of Swedes at Narva. But it was his good luck that his Swedish Majesty, instead of improving so great a victory against him, turned immediately his arms against the King of Poland, against whom he was personally piqued, and that so much the more, inasmuch as he had taken that Prince for one of his best friends, and was just upon the point of concluding with him the strictest alliance when he unexpectedly invaded the Swedish Livonia, and besieged Riga. This was, in all respects, what the Czar could most have wished for; and foreseeing that the longer the war in Poland lasted, the more time should he have both to retrieve his first loss, and to gain Narva, he took care it should be spun out to as great a length as possible; for which end he never sent the King of Poland succour enough to make him too strong for the King of Sweden; who, on the other hand, though he gained one signal victory after the other, yet never could subdue his enemy as long as he received continual reinforcements from his hereditary country. And had not his Swedish Majesty, contrary to most people's expectations, marched directly into Saxony itself, and thereby forced the King of Poland to peace, the Czar would have had leisure enough in all conscience to bring his designs to greater maturity. This peace was one of the greatest disappointments the Czar ever met with, whereby he became singly engaged in the war. He had, however, the comfort of having beforehand taken Narva, and laid a foundation to his favourite town Petersburg, and to the seaport, the docks, and the vast magazines there; all which works, to what perfection they are now brought, let them tell who, with surprise, have seen them.

He (Peter) used all endeavours to bring matters to an accommodation. He proffered very advantageous conditions; Petersburg only, a trifle as he pretended, which he had set his heart upon, he would retain; and even for that he was willing some other way to give satisfaction. But the King of Sweden was too well acquainted with the importance of that place to leave it in the hands of an ambitious prince, and thereby to give him an inlet into the Baltic. This was the only time since the defeat at Narva that the Czar's arms had no other end than that of self-defence. They might, perhaps, even have fallen short therein, had not the King of Sweden (through whose persuasion is still a mystery), instead of marching the shortest way to Novgorod and to Moscow, turned towards Ukrain, where his army, after great losses and sufferings, was at last entirely defeated at Pultowa. As this was a fatal period to the Swedish successes, so how great a deliverance it was to the Muscovites, may be gathered from the Czar's celebrating every year, with great solemnity, the anniversary of that day, from which his ambitious thoughts began to soar still higher. The whole of Livonia, Estland, and the best and greatest part of Finland was now what he demanded, after which, though he might for the present condescend to give peace to the remaining part of Sweden, he knew he could easily even add that to his conquests whenever he pleased. The only obstacle he had to fear in these his projects was from his northern neighbours; but as the Maritime Powers, and even the neighbouring princes in Germany, were then so intent upon their war against France, that they seemed entirely neglectful of that of the North, so there remained only Denmark and Poland to be jealous of. The former of these kingdoms had, ever since King William, of glorious memory, compelled it to make peace with Holstein and, consequently, with Sweden, enjoyed an uninterrupted tranquillity, during which it had time, by a free trade and considerable subsidies from the maritime powers to enrich itself, and was in a condition, by joining itself to Sweden, as it was its interest to do, to stop the Czar's progresses, and timely to prevent its own danger from them. The other, I mean Poland, was now quietly under the government of King Stanislaus, who, owing in a manner his crown to the King of Sweden, could not, out of gratitude, as well as real concern for the interest of his country, fail opposing the designs of a too aspiring neighbour. The Czar was too cunning not to find out a remedy for all this: he represented to the King of Denmark how low the King of Sweden was now brought, and how fair an opportunity he had, during that Prince's long absence, to clip entirely his wings, and to aggrandize himself at his expense. In King Augustus he raised the long-hid resentment for the loss of the Polish Crown, which he told him he might now recover without the least difficulty. Thus both these Princes were immediately caught. The Danes declared war against Sweden without so much as a tolerable pretence, and made a descent upon Schonen, where they were soundly beaten for their pains. King Augustus re-entered Poland, where everything has ever since continued in the greatest disorder, and that in a great measure owing to Muscovite intrigues. It happened, indeed, that these new confederates, whom the Czar had only drawn in to serve his ambition, became at first more necessary to his preservation than he had thought; for the Turks having declared a war against him, they hindered the Swedish arms from joining with them to attack him; but that storm being soon over, through the Czar's wise behaviour and the avarice and folly of the Grand Vizier, he then made the intended use both of these his friends, as well as of them he afterwards, through hopes of gain, persuaded into his alliance, which was to lay all the burthen and hazard of the war upon them, in order entirely to weaken them, together with Sweden, whilst he was preparing himself to swallow the one after the other. He has put them on one difficult attempt after the other; their armies have been considerably lessened by battles and long sieges, whilst his own were either employed in easier conquests, and more profitable to him, or kept at the vast expense of neutral princes—near enough at hand to come up to demand a share of the booty without having struck a blow in getting it. His behaviour has been as cunning at sea, where his fleet has always kept out of harm's way and at a great distance whenever there was any likelihood of an engagement between the Danes and the Swedes. He hoped that when these two nations had ruined one another's fleets, his might then ride master in the Baltic. All this while he had taken care to make his men improve, by the example of foreigners and under their command, in the art of war.... His fleets will soon considerably outnumber the Swedish and the Danish ones joined together. He need not fear their being a hindrance from his giving a finishing stroke to this great and glorious undertaking. Which done, let us look to ourselves; he will then most certainly become our rival, and as dangerous to us as he is now neglected. We then may, perhaps, though too late, call to mind what our own ministers and merchants have told us of his designs of carrying on alone all the northern trade, and of getting all that from Turkey and Persia into his hands through the rivers which he is joining and making navigable from the Caspian, or the Black Sea, to his Petersburg. We shall then wonder at our blindness that we did not suspect his designs when we heard the prodigious works he has done at Petersburg and Revel; of which last place, the Daily Courant, dated November 23, says:

"Hague, Nov. 17.

"The captains of the men-of-war of the States, who have been at Revel, advise that the Czar has put that port and the fortifications of the place into such a condition of defence that it may pass for one of the most considerable fortresses, not only of the Baltic, but even of Europe."

Leave we him now, as to his sea affairs, commerce and manufactures, and other works both of his policy and power, and let us view him in regard to his proceedings in this last campaign, especially as to that so much talked of descent, he, in conjunction with his allies, was to make upon Schonen, and we shall find that even therein he has acted with his usual cunning. There is no doubt but the King of Denmark was the first that proposed this descent. He found that nothing but a speedy end to a war he had so rashly and unjustly begun, could save his country from ruin and from the bold attempts of the King of Sweden, either against Norway, or against Zealand and Copenhagen. To treat separately with that prince was a thing he could not do, as foreseeing that he would not part with an inch of ground to so unfair an enemy; and he was afraid that a Congress for a general place, supposing the King of Sweden would consent to it upon the terms proposed by his enemies, would draw the negotiations out beyond what the situation of his affairs could bear. He invites, therefore, all his confederates to make a home thrust at the King of Sweden, by a descent into his country, where, having defeated him, as by the superiority of the forces to be employed in that design he hoped they should, they might force him to an immediate peace on such terms as they themselves pleased. I don't know how far the rest of his confederates came into that project; but neither the Prussian nor the Hanoverian Court appeared openly in that project, and how far our English fleet, under Sir John Norris, was to have forwarded it, I have nothing to say, but leave others to judge out of the King of Denmark's own declaration: but the Czar came readily into it. He got thereby a new pretence to carry the war one campaign more at other people's expense; to march his troops into the Empire again, and to have them quartered and maintained, first in Mecklenburg and then in Zealand. In the meantime he had his eyes upon Wismar, and upon a Swedish island called Gotland. If, by surprise, he could get the first out of the hands of his confederates, he then had a good seaport, whither to transport his troops when he pleased into Germany, without asking the King of Prussia's leave for a free passage through his territories; and if, by a sudden descent, he could dislodge the Swedes out of the other, he then became master of the best port in the Baltic. He miscarried, however, in both these projects; for Wismar was too well guarded to be surprised; and he found his confederates would not give him a helping hand towards conquering Gotland. After this he began to look with another eye upon the descent to be made upon Schonen. He found it equally contrary to his interest, whether it succeeded or not. For if he did, and the King was thereby forced to a general peace, he knew his interests therein would be least regarded; having already notice enough of his confederates being ready to sacrifice them, provided they got their own terms. If he did not succeed, then, besides the loss of the flower of an army he had trained and disciplined with so much care, as he very well foresaw that the English fleet would hinder the King of Sweden from attempting anything against Denmark; so he justly feared the whole shock would fall upon him, and he be thereby forced to surrender all he had taken from Sweden. These considerations made him entirely resolved not to make one of the descent; but he did not care to declare it till as late as possible: first, that he might the longer have his troops maintained at the Danish expense; secondly, that it might be too late for the King of Denmark to demand the necessary troops from his other confederates, and to make the descent without him; and, lastly, that by putting the Dane to a vast expense in making necessary preparations, he might still weaken him more, and, therefore, make him now the more dependent on him, and hereafter a more easy prey.

Thus he very carefully dissembles his real thoughts, till just when the descent was to be made, and then he, all of a sudden, refuses joining it, and defers it till next spring, with this averment, that he will then be as good as his word. But mark him, as some of our newspapers tell us, under this restriction, unless he can get an advantageous peace of Sweden. This passage, together with the common report we now have of his treating a separate peace with the King of Sweden, is a new instance of his cunning and policy. He has there two strings to his bow, of which one must serve his turn. There is no doubt but the Czar knows that an accommodation between him and the King of Sweden must be very difficult to bring about. For as he, on the one side, should never consent to part with those seaports, for the getting of which he began this war, and which are absolutely necessary towards carrying on his great and vast designs; so the King of Sweden would look upon it as directly contrary to his interest to yield up these same seaports, if possibly he could hinder it. But then again, the Czar is so well acquainted with the great and heroic spirit of his Swedish Majesty, that he does not question his yielding, rather in point of interest than nicety of honour. From hence it is, he rightly judges, that his Swedish Majesty must be less exasperated against him who, though he began an unjust war, has very often paid dearly for it, and carried it on all along through various successes than against some confederates; that taking an opportunity of his Swedish Majesty's misfortunes, fell upon him in an ungenerous manner, and made a partition treaty of his provinces. The Czar, still more to accommodate himself to the genius of his great enemy, unlike his confederates, who, upon all occasions, spared no reflections and even very unbecoming ones (bullying memorials and hectoring manifestoes), spoke all along with the utmost civility of his brother Charles as he calls him, maintains him to be the greatest general in Europe, and even publicly avers, he will more trust a word from him than the greatest assurances, oaths, nay, even treaties with his confederates. These kind of civilities may, perhaps, make a deeper impression upon the noble mind of the King of Sweden, and he be persuaded rather to sacrifice a real interest to a generous enemy, than to gratify, in things of less moment, those by whom he has been ill, and even inhumanly used. But if this should not succeed, the Czar is still a gainer by having made his confederates uneasy at these his separate negotiations; and as we find by the newspapers, the more solicitous to keep him ready to their confederacy, which must cost them very large proffers and promises. In the meantime he leaves the Dane and the Swede securely bound up together in war, and weakening one another as fast as they can, and he turns towards the Empire and views the Protestant Princes there; and, under many specious pretences, not only marches and counter-marches about their several territories his troops that came back from Denmark, but makes also slowly advance towards Germany those whom he has kept this great while in Poland, under pretence to help the King against his dissatisfied subjects, whose commotions all the while he was the greatest fomenter of. He considers the Emperor is in war with the Turks, and therefore has found, by too successful experience, how little his Imperial Majesty is able to show his authority in protecting the members of the Empire. His troops remain in Mecklenburg, notwithstanding their departure is highly insisted upon. His replies to all the demands on that subject are filled with such reasons as if he would give new laws to the Empire.

Now let us suppose that the King of Sweden should think it more honourable to make a peace with the Czar, and to carry the force of his resentment against his less generous enemies, what a stand will then the princes of the empire, even those that unadvisedly drew in 40,000 Muscovites, to secure the tranquillity of that empire against 10,000 or 12,000 Swedes,—I say what stand will they be able to make against him while the Emperor is already engaged in war with the Turks? and the Poles, when they are once in peace among themselves (if after the miseries of so long a war they are in a condition to undertake anything) are by treaty obliged to join their aids against that common enemy of Christianity.

Some will say I make great and sudden rises from very small beginnings. My answer is, that I would have such an objector look back and reflect why I show him, from such a speck of entity, at his first origin, growing, through more improbable and almost insuperable difficulties, to such a bulk as he has already attained to, and whereby, as his advocates, the Dutch themselves own, he is grown too formidable for the repose, not only of his neighbours, but of Europe in general.

But then, again, they will say he has no pretence either to make a peace with the Swede separately from the Dane or to make war upon other princes, some of whom he is bound in alliance with. Whoever thinks these objections not answered must have considered the Czar neither as to his nature or to his ends. The Dutch own further, that he made war against Sweden without any specious pretence. He that made war without any specious pretence may make a peace without any specious pretence, and make a new war without any specious pretence for it too. His Imperial Majesty (of Austria), like a wise Prince, when he was obliged to make war with the Ottomans, made it, as in policy, he should, powerfully. But, in the meantime, may not the Czar, who is a wise and potent Prince too, follow the example upon the neighbouring Princes round him that are Protestants? If he should, I tremble to speak it, it is not impossible, but in this age of Christianity the Protestant religion should, in a great measure, be abolished; and that among the Christians, the Greeks and Romans may once more come to be the only Pretenders for Universal Empire. The pure possibility carries with it warning enough for the Maritime Powers, and all the other Protestant Princes, to mediate a peace for Sweden, and strengthen his arms again, without which no preparations can put them sufficiently upon their guard; and this must be done early and betimes, before the King of Sweden, either out of despair or revenge, throws himself into the Czar's hands. For 'tis a certain maxim (which all Princes ought, and the Czar seems at this time to observe too much for the repose of Christendom) that a wise man must not stand for ceremony, and only turn with opportunities. No, he must even run with them. For the Czar's part, I will venture to say so much in his commendation, that he will hardly suffer himself to be overtaken that way. He seems to act just as the tide serves. There is nothing which contributes more to the making our undertakings prosperous than the taking of times and opportunities; for time carrieth with it the seasons of opportunities of business. If you let them slip, all your designs are rendered unsuccessful.

In short, things seem now come to that crisis that peace should as soon as possible be procured to the Swede, with such advantageous articles as are consistent with the nicety of his honour to accept, and with the safety of the Protestant interest, that he should have offered to him, which can be scarce less than all the possessions which he formerly had in the Empire. As in all other things, so in politics, a long-tried certainty must be preferred before an uncertainty, tho' grounded on ever so probable suppositions. Now can there be anything more certain, than that the provinces Sweden has had in the Empire, were given to it to make it the nearer at hand and the better able to secure the Protestant interest, which, together with the liberties of the Empire it just then had saved? Can there be anything more certain than that that kingdom has, by those means, upon all occasions, secured that said interest now near fourscore years? Can there be anything more certain than, as to his present Swedish Majesty, that I may use the words of a letter her late Majesty, Queen Anne, wrote to him (Charles XII.), and in the time of a Whig Ministry too, viz.: "That, as a true Prince, hero and Christian, the chief end of his endeavours has been the promotion of the fear of God among men: and that without insisting on his own particular interest."

On the other hand, is it not very uncertain whether those princes, who, by sharing among them the Swedish provinces in the Empire, are now going to set up as protectors of the Protestant interests there, exclusive of the Swedes, will be able to do it? Denmark is already so low, and will in all appearance be so much lower still before the end of the war, that very little assistance can be expected from it in a great many years. In Saxony, the prospect is but too dismal under a Popish prince, so that there remain only the two illustrious houses of Hanover and Brandenburg of all the Protestant princes, powerful enough to lead the rest. Let us therefore only make a parallel between what now happens in the Duchy of Mecklenburg, and what may happen to the Protestant interest, and we shall soon find how we may be mistaken in our reckoning. That said poor Duchy has been most miserably ruined by the Muscovite troops, and it is still so; the Electors of Brandenburg and Hanover are obliged, both as directors of the circle of Lower Saxony, as neighbours, and Protestant Princes, to rescue a fellow state of the Empire, and a Protestant country, from so cruel an oppression of a foreign Power. But, pray, what have they done? The Elector of Brandenburg, cautious lest the Muscovites might on one side invade his electorate, and on the other side from Livonia and Poland, his kingdom of Prussia; and the Elector of Hanover having the same wise caution as to his hereditary countries, have not upon this, though very pressing occasion, thought it for their interest, to use any other means than representations. But pray with what success? The Muscovites are still in Mecklenburg, and if at last they march out of it, it will be when the country is so ruined that they cannot there subsist any longer.

It seems the King of Sweden should be restored to all that he has lost on the side of the Czar; and this appears the joint interest of both the Maritime Powers. This may they please to undertake: Holland, because it is a maxim there "that the Czar grows too great, and must not be suffered to settle in the Baltic, and that Sweden must not be abandoned"; Great Britain, because, if the Czar compasses his vast and prodigious views, he will, by the ruin and conquest of Sweden, become our nearer and more dreadful neighbour. Besides, we are bound to it by a treaty concluded in the year 1700, between King William and the present King of Sweden, by virtue of which King William assisted the King of Sweden, when in more powerful circumstances, with all that he desired, with great sums of money, several hundred pieces of cloth, and considerable quantities of gunpowder.

But some Politicians (whom nothing can make jealous of the growing strength and abilities of the Czar) though they are even foxes and vulpones in the art, either will not see or pretend they cannot see how the Czar can ever be able to make so great a progress in power as to hurt us here in our island. To them it is easy to repeat the same answer a hundred times over, if they would be so kind as to take it at last, viz., that what has been may be again; and that they did not see how he could reach the height of power, which he has already arrived at, after, I must confess, a very incredible manner. Let those incredulous people look narrowly into the nature and the ends and the designs of this great monarch; they will find that they are laid very deep, and that his plans carry in them a prodigious deal of prudence and foresight, and his ends are at the long run brought about by a kind of magic in policy; and will they not after that own that we ought to fear everything from him? As he desires that the designs with which he labours may not prove abortive, so he does not assign them a certain day of their birth, but leaves them to the natural productions of fit times and occasions, like those curious artists in China, who temper the mould this day of which a vessel may be made a hundred years hence.

There is another sort of short-sighted politicians among us, who have more of cunning court intrigue and immediate statecraft in them than of true policy and concern for their country's interest. These gentlemen pin entirely their faith upon other people's sleeves; ask as to everything that is proposed to them, how it is liked at Court? what the opinion of their party is concerning it? and if the contrary party is for or against it? Hereby they rule their judgment, and it is enough for their cunning leaders to brand anything with Whiggism or Jacobitism, for to make these people, without any further inquiry into the matter, blindly espouse it or oppose it. This, it seems, is at present the case of the subject we are upon. Anything said or written in favour of Sweden and the King thereof, is immediately said to come from a Jacobite pen, and thus reviled and rejected, without being read or considered. Nay, I have heard gentlemen go so far as to maintain publicly, and with all the vehemence in the world, that the King of Sweden was a Roman Catholic, and that the Czar was a good Protestant. This, indeed, is one of the greatest misfortunes our country labours under, and till we begin to see with our own eyes, and inquire ourselves into the truth of things, we shall be led away, God knows whither, at last. The serving of Sweden according to our treaties and real interest has nothing to do with our party causes. Instead of seeking for and taking hold of any pretence to undo

Sweden, we ought openly to assist it. Could our Protestant succession have a better friend or a bolder champion?

I shall conclude this by thus shortly recapitulating what I have said. That since the Czar has not only replied to the King of Denmark entreating the contrary, but also answered our Admiral Norris, that he would persist in his resolution to delay the descent upon Schonen, and is said by other newspapers to resolve not to make it then, if he can have peace with Sweden; every Prince, and we more particularly, ought to be jealous of his having some such design as I mention in view, and consult how to prevent them, and to clip, in time, his too aspiring wings, which cannot be effectually done, first, without the Maritime Powers please to begin to keep him in some check and awe, and 'tis to be hoped a certain potent nation, that has helped him forward, can, in some measure, bring him back, and may then speak to this great enterpriser in the language of a countryman in Spain, who coming to an image enshrined, the first making whereof he could well remember, and not finding all the respectful usage he expected,—"You need not," quoth he, "be so proud, for we have known you from a plum-tree." The next only way is to restore, by a peace, to the King of Sweden what he has lost; that checks his (the Czar's) power immediately, and on that side nothing else can. I wish it may not at last be found true, that those who have been fighting against that King have, in the main, been fighting against themselves. If the Swede ever has his dominions again, and lowers the high spirit of the Czar, still he may say by his neighbours, as an old Greek hero did, whom his countrymen constantly sent into exile whenever he had done them a service, but were forced to call him back to their aid, whenever they wanted success. "These people," quoth he, "are always using me like the palm-tree. They will be breaking my branches continually, and yet, if there comes a storm, they run to me, and can't find a better place for shelter." But if he has them not, I shall only exclaim a phrase out of Terence's "Andria":

"Hoccine credibile est aut memorabile
Tanta vecordia innata cuiquam ut siet,
Ut malis gaudeant?"
4. Postscript.—I flatter myself that this little history is of that curious nature, and on matters hitherto so unobserved, that I consider it, with pride, as a valuable New Year's gift to the present world; and that posterity will accept it, as the like, for many years after, and read it over on that anniversary, and call it their Warning Piece. I must have my Exegi-Monumentum as well as others.

FOOTNOTE:

[20] Or, to follow this affectation of silliness into more recent times, is there anything in diplomatic history that could match Lord Palmerston's proposal made to Marshal Soult (in 1839), to storm the Dardanelles, in order to afford the Sultan the support of the Anglo-French fleet against Russia?

CHAPTER III

To understand a limited historical epoch, we must step beyond its limits, and compare it with other historical epochs. To judge Governments and their acts, we must measure them by their own times and the conscience of their contemporaries. Nobody will condemn a British statesman of the 17th century for acting on a belief in witchcraft, if he find Bacon himself ranging demonology in the catalogue of science. On the other hand, if the Stanhopes, the Walpoles, the Townshends, etc., were suspected, opposed, and denounced in their own country by their own contemporaries as tools or accomplices of Russia, it will no longer do to shelter their policy behind the convenient screen of prejudice and ignorance common to their time. At the head of the historical evidence we have to sift, we place, therefore, long-forgotten English pamphlets printed at the very time of Peter I. These preliminary pièces des procès we shall, however, limit to three pamphlets, which, from three different points of view, illustrate the conduct of England towards Sweden. The first, the Northern Crisis (given in Chapter II.), revealing the general system of Russia, and the dangers accruing to England from the Russification of Sweden; the second, called The Defensive Treaty, judging the acts of England by the Treaty of 1700; and the third, entitled Truth is but Truth, however it is Timed, proving that the new-fangled schemes which magnified Russia into the paramount Power of the Baltic were in flagrant opposition to the traditional policy England had pursued during the course of a whole century.

The pamphlet called The Defensive Treaty bears no date of publication. Yet in one passage it states that, for reinforcing the Danish fleet, eight English men-of-war were left at Copenhagen "the year before the last," and in another passage alludes to the assembling of the confederate fleet for the Schonen expedition as having occurred "last summer." As the former event took place in 1715, and the latter towards the end of the summer of 1716, it is evident that the pamphlet was written and published in the earlier part of the year 1717. The Defensive Treaty between England and Sweden, the single articles of which the pamphlet comments upon in the form of queries, was concluded in 1700 between William III. and Charles XII., and was not to expire before 1719. Yet, during almost the whole of this period, we find England continually assisting Russia and waging war against Sweden, either by secret intrigue or open force, although the treaty was never rescinded nor war ever declared. This fact is, perhaps, even less strange than the conspiration de silence under which modern historians have succeeded in burying it, and among them historians by no means sparing of censure against the British Government of that time, for having, without any previous declaration of war, destroyed the Spanish fleet in the Sicilian waters. But then, at least, England was not bound to Spain by a defensive treaty. How, then, are we to explain this contrary treatment of similar cases? The piracy committed against Spain was one of the weapons which the Whig Ministers, seceding from the Cabinet in 1717, caught hold of to harass their remaining colleagues. When the latter stepped forward in 1718, and urged Parliament to declare war against Spain, Sir Robert Walpole rose from his seat in the Commons, and in a most virulent speech denounced the late ministerial acts "as contrary to the laws of nations, and a breach of solemn treaties." "Giving sanction to them in the manner proposed," he said, "could have no other view than to screen ministers, who were conscious of having done something amiss, and who, having begun a war against Spain, would now make it the Parliament's war." The treachery against Sweden and the connivance at the plans of Russia, never happening to afford the ostensible pretext for a family quarrel amongst the Whig rulers (they being rather unanimous on these points), never obtained the honours of historical criticism so lavishly spent upon the Spanish incident.

How apt modern historians generally are to receive their cue from the official tricksters themselves, is best shown by their reflections on the commercial interests of England with respect to Russia and Sweden. Nothing has been more exaggerated than the dimensions of the trade opened to Great Britain by the huge market of the Russia of Peter the Great, and his immediate successors. Statements bearing not the slightest touch of criticism have been allowed to creep from one book-shelf to another, till they became at last historical household furniture, to be inherited by every successive historian, without even the beneficium inventarii. Some incontrovertible statistical figures will suffice to blot out these hoary common-places.

24

British Commerce from 1697-1700.

	£
Export to Russia	58,884
Import from Russia	112,252
Total	171,136

Export to Sweden	57,555
Import from Sweden	212,094
Total	269,649

During the same period the total

	£
Export of England amounted to	3,525,906
Import	3,482,586
Total	7,008,492

In 1716, after all the Swedish provinces in the Baltic, and on the Gulfs of Finland and Bothnia, had fallen into the hands of Peter I., the

	£
Export to Russia was	113,154
Import from Russia	197,270
Total	310,424

Export to Sweden 24,101	
Import from Sweden	136,959
Total	161,060

At the same time, the total of English exports and imports together reached about £10,000,000. It will be seen from these figures, when compared with those of 1697-1700, that the increase in the Russian trade is balanced by the decrease in the Swedish trade, and that what was added to the one was subtracted from the other.

In 1730, the

	£
Export to Russia was	46,275
Import from Russia	258,802
Total	305,077

Fifteen years, then, after the consolidation in the meanwhile of the Muscovite settlement on the Baltic, the British trade with Russia had fallen off by £5,347. The general trade of England reaching in 1730 the sum of £16,329,001, the Russian trade amounted not yet to 1/53rd of its total value. Again, thirty years later, in 1760, the account between Great Britain and Russia stands thus:

25

	£
Import from Russia (in 1760)	536,504
Export to Russia	39,761
Total	£576,265

while the general trade of England amounted to £26,361,760. Comparing these figures with those of 1706, we find that the total of the Russian commerce, after nearly half a century, has increased by the trifling sum of only £265,841. That England suffered positive loss by her new commercial relations with Russia under Peter I. and Catherine I. becomes evident on comparing, on the one side, the export and import figures, and on the other, the sums expended on the frequent naval expeditions to the Baltic which England undertook during the lifetime of Charles XII., in order to break down his resistance to Russia, and, after his death, on the professed necessity of checking the maritime encroachments of Russia.

Another glance at the statistical data given for the years 1697, 1700, 1716, 1730, and 1760, will show that the British export trade to Russia was continually falling off, save in 1716, when Russia engrossed the whole Swedish trade on the eastern coast of the Baltic and the Gulf of Bothnia, and had not yet found the opportunity of subjecting it to her own regulations. From £58,884, at which the British exports to Russia stood during 1697-1700, when Russia was still precluded from the Baltic, they had sunk to £46,275 in 1730, and to £39,761 in 1760, showing a decrease of £19,123, or about 1/3rd of their original amount in 1700. If, then, since, the absorption of the Swedish provinces by Russia, the British market proved expanding for Russia raw produce, the Russian market, on its side, proved straitening for British manufacturers, a feature of that trade which could hardly recommend it at a time when the Balance of Trade doctrine ruled supreme. To trace the circumstances which produced the increase of the Anglo-Russian trade under Catherine II. would lead us too far from the period we are considering.

On the whole, then, we arrive at the following conclusions: During the first sixty years of the eighteenth century the total Anglo-Russian trade formed but a very diminutive fraction of the general trade of England, say less than 1/45th. Its sudden increase during the earliest years of Peter's sway over the Baltic did not at all affect the general balance of British trade, as it was a simple transfer from its Swedish account to its Russian account. In the later times of Peter I., as well as under his immediate successors, Catherine I. and Anne, the Anglo-Russian trade was positively declining; during the whole epoch, dating from the final settlement of Russia in the Baltic provinces, the export of British manufactures to Russia was continually falling off, so that at its end it stood one-third lower than at its beginning, when that trade was still confined to the port of Archangel. Neither the contemporaries of Peter I., nor the next British generation reaped any benefit from the advancement of Russia to the Baltic. In general the Baltic trade of Great Britain was at that time trifling in regard of the capital involved, but important in regard of its character. It afforded England the raw produce for its maritime stores. That from the latter point of view the Baltic was in safer keeping in the hands of Sweden than in those of Russia, was not only proved by the pamphlets we are reprinting, but fully understood by the British Ministers themselves. Stanhope writing, for instance, to Townshend on October 16th, 1716:

"It is certain that if the Czar be let alone three years, he will be absolute master in those seas."[21]

If, then, neither the navigation nor the general commerce of England was interested in the treacherous support given to Russia against Sweden, there existed, indeed, one small fraction of British merchants whose interests were identical with the Russian ones—the Russian Trade Company. It was this gentry that raised a cry against Sweden. See, for instance:

"Several grievances of the English merchants in their trade into the dominions of the King of Sweden, whereby it does appear how dangerous it may be for the English nation to depend on Sweden only for the supply of the naval stores, when they might be amply furnished with the like stores from the dominions of the Emperor of Russia."

"The case of the merchants trading to Russia" (a petition to Parliament), etc.

It was they who in the years 1714, 1715, and 1716, regularly assembled twice a week before the opening of Parliament, to draw up in public meetings the complaints of the British merchantmen against Sweden. On this small fraction the Ministers relied; they were even busy in getting up its demonstrations, as may be seen from the letters addressed by Count Gyllenborg to Baron Görtz, dated 4th of November and 4th of December, 1716, wanting, as they did, but the shadow of a pretext to drive their "mercenary Parliament," as Gyllenborg calls it, where they liked. The influence of these British merchants trading to Russia was again exhibited in the year 1765, and our own times have witnessed the working for his interest, of a Russian merchant at the head of the Board of Trade, and of a Chancellor of the Exchequer in the interest of a cousin engaged in the Archangel trade.

The oligarchy which, after the "glorious revolution," usurped wealth and power at the cost of the mass of the British people, was, of course, forced to look out for allies, not only abroad, but also at home. The latter they found in what the French would call la haute bourgeoisie, as represented by the Bank of England, the money-lenders, State creditors, East India and other trading corporations, the great manufacturers, etc. How tenderly they managed the material interests of that class may be learned from the whole of their domestic legislation— Bank Acts, Protectionist enactments, Poor Regulations, etc. As to their foreign policy, they wanted to give it the appearance at least of being altogether regulated by the mercantile interest, an appearance the more easily to be produced, as the exclusive interest of one or the other small fraction of that class would, of course, be always identified with this or that Ministerial measure. The interested fraction then raised the commerce and navigation cry, which the nation stupidly re-echoed.

At that time, then, there devolved on the Cabinet, at least, the onus of inventing mercantile pretexts, however futile, for their measures of foreign policy. In our own epoch, British Ministers have thrown this burden on foreign nations, leaving to the French, the Germans, etc., the irksome task of discovering the secret and hidden mercantile springs of their actions. Lord Palmerston, for instance, takes a step apparently the most damaging to the material interests of Great Britain. Up starts a State philosopher, on the other side of the Atlantic, or of the Channel, or in the heart of Germany, who puts his head to the rack to dig out the mysteries of the mercantile Machiavelism of "perfide Albion," of which Palmerston is supposed the unscrupulous and unflinching executor. We will, en passant, show, by a few modern instances, what desperate shifts those foreigners have been driven to, who feel themselves obliged to interpret Palmerston's acts by what they imagine to be the English commercial policy. In his valuable Histoire Politique et Sociale des Principautés Danubiennes, M. Elias Regnault, startled by the Russian conduct, before and during the years 1848-49 of Mr. Colquhoun, the British Consul at Bucharest, suspects that England has some secret material interest in keeping down the trade of the Principalities. The late Dr. Cunibert, private physician of old Milosh, in his most interesting account of the Russian intrigues in Servia, gives a curious relation of the manner in which Lord Palmerston, through the instrumentality of Colonel Hodges, betrayed Milosh to Russia by feigning to support him against her. Fully

27

believing in the personal integrity of Hodges, and the patriotic zeal of Palmerston, Dr. Cunibert is found to go a step further than M. Elias Regnault. He suspects England of being interested in putting down Turkish commerce generally. General Mieroslawski, in his last work on Poland, is not very far from intimating that mercantile Machiavelism instigated England to sacrifice her own prestige in Asia Minor, by the surrender of Kars. As a last instance may serve the present lucubrations of the Paris papers, hunting after the secret springs of commercial jealousy, which induce Palmerston to oppose the cutting of the Isthmus of Suez canal.

To return to our subject. The mercantile pretext hit upon by the Townshends, Stanhopes, etc., for the hostile demonstrations against Sweden, was the following. Towards the end of 1713, Peter I. had ordered all the hemp and other produce of his dominions, destined for export, to be carried to St. Petersburg instead of Archangel. Then the Swedish Regency, during the absence of Charles XII., and Charles XII. himself, after his return from Bender, declared all the Baltic ports, occupied by the Russians, to be blockaded. Consequently, English ships, breaking through the blockade, were confiscated. The English Ministry then asserted that British merchantmen had the right of trading to those ports according to Article XVII. of the Defensive Treaty of 1700, by which English commerce, with the exception of contraband of war, was allowed to go on with ports of the enemy. The absurdity and falsehood of this pretext being fully exposed in the pamphlet we are about to reprint, we will only remark that the case had been more than once decided against commercial nations, not bound, like England, by treaty to defend the integrity of the Swedish Empire. In the year 1561, when the Russians took Narva, and laboured hard to establish their commerce there, the Hanse towns, chiefly Lübeck, tried to possess themselves of this traffic. Eric XIV., then King of Sweden, resisted their pretensions. The city of Lübeck represented this resistance as altogether new, as they had carried on their commerce with the Russians time out of mind, and pleaded the common right of nations to navigate in the Baltic, provided their vessels carried no contraband of war. The King replied that he did not dispute the Hanse towns the liberty of trading with Russia, but only with Narva, which was no Russian port. In the year 1579 again, the Russians having broken the suspension of arms with Sweden, the Danes likewise claimed the navigation to Narva, by virtue of their treaty, but King John was as firm in maintaining the contrary, as was his brother Eric.

In her open demonstrations of hostility against the King of Sweden, as well as in the false pretence on which they were founded, England seemed only to follow in the track of Holland, which declaring the confiscation of its ships to be piracy, had issued two proclamations against Sweden in 1714.

In one respect, the case of the States-General was the same as that of England. King William had concluded the Defensive Treaty as well for Holland as for England. Besides, Article XVI., in the Treaty of Commerce, concluded between Holland and Sweden in 1703, expressly stipulated that no navigation ought to be allowed to the ports blocked up by either of the confederates. The then common Dutch cant that "there was no hindering traders from carrying their merchandise where they will," was the more impudent as, during the war, ending with the Peace of Ryswick, the Dutch Republic had declared all France to be blocked up, forbidden the neutral Powers all trade with that kingdom, and caused all their ships that went there or came thence to be brought up without any regard to the nature of their cargoes.

In another respect, the situation of Holland was different from that of England. Fallen from its commercial and maritime grandeur, Holland had then already entered upon its epoch of decline. Like Genoa and Venice, when new roads of commerce had dispossessed them of their old mercantile supremacy, it was forced to lend out to other nations its capital, grown too large for the vessels of its own commerce. Its fatherland had begun to lie there where the best interest for its capital was paid. Russia, therefore, proved an immense market, less for the commerce than for the outlay of capital and men. To this moment Holland has remained the banker of Russia. At the time of Peter they supplied Russia with ships, officers, arms, and money, so that his fleet, as a contemporary writer remarks, ought to have been called a Dutch rather than a Muscovite one. They gloried in having sent the first European merchant ship to St. Petersburg, and returned the commercial privileges they had obtained from Peter, or hoped to obtain from him, by that fawning meanness which characterizes their intercourse with Japan. Here, then, was quite another solid foundation than in England for the Russianism of statesmen, whom Peter I. had entrapped during his stay at Amsterdam, and the Hague in 1697, whom he afterwards directed by his ambassadors, and with whom he renewed his personal influence during his renewed stay at Amsterdam in 1716-17. Yet, if the paramount influence England exercised over Holland during the first decennia of the 18th century be considered, there can remain no doubt that the proclamations against Sweden by the States-General would never have been issued, if not with the previous consent and at the instigation of England. The intimate connection between the English and Dutch Governments served more than once the former to put up precedents in the name of Holland, which they were resolved to act upon in the name of England. On the other hand, it is no less certain that the Dutch statesmen were employed by the Czar to influence the British ones. Thus Horace Walpole, the brother of the "Father of Corruption," the brother-in-law of the Minister, Townshend, and the British Ambassador at the Hague during 1715-16, was evidently inveigled into the Russian interest by his Dutch friends. Thus, as we shall see by-and-by, Theyls, the Secretary to the Dutch Embassy at Constantinople, at the most critical period of the deadly struggle between Charles XII. and Peter I., managed affairs at the same time for the Embassies of England and Holland at the Sublime Porte. This Theylls, in a print of his, openly claims it as a merit with his nation to have been the devoted and rewarded agent of Russian intrigue.

FOOTNOTE:

[21] In the year 1657, when the Courts of Denmark and Brandenburg intended engaging the Muscovites to fall upon Sweden, they instructed their Minister so to manage the affair that the Czar might by no means get any footing in the Baltic, because "they did not know what to do with so troublesome a neighbour." (See Puffendorf's History of Brandenburg.)

CHAPTER IV

"The Defensive Treaty concluded in the year 1700, between his late Majesty, King William, of ever-glorious memory, and his present Swedish Majesty, King Charles XII. Published at the earnest desire of several members of both Houses of Parliament.

'Nec rumpite fœdera pacis,
Nec regnis præferte fidem.'
—Silius, Lip. II.
"Article I. Establishes between the Kings of Sweden and England 'a sincere and constant friendship for ever, a league and good correspondence, so that they shall never mutually or separately molest one another's kingdoms, provinces, colonies, or subjects, wheresoever situated, nor shall they suffer or agree that this should be done by others, etc.'

"Article II. 'Moreover, each of the Allies, his heirs and successors, shall be obliged to take care of, and promote, as much as in him lies, the profit and honour of the other, to detect and give notice to his other ally (as soon as it shall come to his own knowledge) of all imminent dangers, conspiracies, and hostile designs formed against him, to withstand them as much as possible, and to prevent them both by advice and assistance; and therefore it shall not be lawful for either of the Allies, either by themselves or any other whatsoever, to act, treat, or endeavour anything to the prejudice or loss of the other, his lands or dominions whatsoever or wheresoever, whether by land or sea; that one shall in no wise favour the other's foes, either rebels or enemies, to the prejudice of his Ally,' etc.

"Query I. How the words marked in italics agree with our present conduct, when our fleet acts in conjunction with the enemies of Sweden, the Czar commands our fleet, our Admiral enters into Councils of War, and is not only privy to all their designs, but together with our own Minister at Copenhagen (as the King of Denmark has himself owned it in a public declaration), pushed on the Northern Confederates to an enterprise entirely destructive to our Ally Sweden, I mean the descent designed last summer upon Schonen?

"Query II. In what manner we also must explain that passage in the first article by which it is stipulated that one Ally shall not either by themselves or any other whatsoever, act, treat, or endeavour anything to the loss of the other's lands and dominions; to justify in particular our leaving in the year 1715, even when the season was so far advanced as no longer to admit of our usual pretence of conveying and protecting our trade, which was then got already safe home, eight men-of-war in the Baltic, with orders to join in one line of battle with the Danes, whereby we made them so much superior in number to the Swedish fleet, that it could not come to the relief of Straelsund, and whereby we chiefly occasioned Sweden's entirely losing its German Provinces, and even the extreme danger his Swedish Majesty ran in his own person, in crossing the sea, before the surrender of the town.

"Article III. By a special defensive treaty, the Kings of Sweden and England mutually oblige themselves, 'in a strict alliance, to defend one another mutually, as well as their kingdoms, territories, provinces, states, subjects, possessions, as their rights and liberties of navigation and commerce, as well in the Northern, Deucalidonian, Western, and Britannic Sea, commonly called the Channel, the Baltic, the Sound; as also of the privileges and prerogatives of each of the Allies belonging to them, by virtue of treaties and agreements, as well as by received customs, the laws of nations, hereditary right, against any aggressors or invaders and molesters in Europe by sea or land, etc.'

"Query. It being by the law of nations an indisputable right and prerogative of any king or people, in case of a great necessity or threatening ruin, to use all such means they themselves shall judge most necessary for their preservation; it having moreover been a constant prerogative and practice of the Swedes, for these several hundred years, in case of a war with their most dreadful enemies the Muscovites, to hinder all trade with them in the Baltic; and since it is also stipulated in this article that amongst other things, one Ally ought to defend the prerogatives belonging to the other, even by received customs, and the law of nations: how come we now, the King of Sweden stands more than ever in need of using that prerogative, not only to dispute it, but also to take thereof a pretence for an open hostility against him?

"Articles IV., V., VI., and VII. fix the strength of the auxiliary forces England and Sweden are to send each other in case the territory of either of these powers should be invaded, or its navigation 'molested or hindered' in one of the seas enumerated in Article III. The invasion of the German provinces of Sweden is expressly included as a casus fœderis.

"Article VIII. stipulates that that Ally who is not attacked shall first act the part of a pacific mediator; but, the mediation having proved a failure, 'the aforesaid forces shall be sent without delay; nor shall the confederates desist before the injured party shall be satisfied in all things.'

"Article IX. That Ally that requires the stipulated 'help, has to choose whether he will have the above-named army either all or any, either in soldiers, ships, ammunition, or money.'

"Article X. Ships and armies serve under 'the command of him that required them.'

"Article XI. 'But if it should happen that the above-mentioned forces should not be proportionable to the danger, as supposing that perhaps the aggressor should be assisted by the forces of some other confederates of his, then one of the Allies, after previous request, shall be obliged to help the other that is injured, with greater forces, such as he shall be able to raise with safety and convenience, both by sea and land....'

"Article XII. 'It shall be lawful for either of the Allies and their subjects to bring their men-of-war into one another's harbours, and to winter there.' Peculiar negotiations about this point shall take place at Stockholm, but 'in the meanwhile, the articles of treaty concluded at London, 1661, relating to the navigation and commerce shall remain, in their full force, as much as if they were inserted here word for word.'

"Article XIII. ' ... The subjects of either of the Allies ... shall no way, either by sea or land, serve them (the enemies of either of the Allies), either as mariners or soldiers, and therefore it shall be forbid them upon severe penalty.'

"Article XIV. 'If it happens that either of the confederate kings ... should be engaged in a war against a common enemy, or be molested by any other neighbouring king ... in his own kingdoms or provinces ... to the hindering of which, he that requires help may by the force of this treaty himself be obliged to send help: then that Ally so molested shall not be obliged to send the promised help....'

"Query I. Whether in our conscience we don't think the King of Sweden most unjustly attacked by all his enemies; whether consequently we are not convinced that we owe him the assistance stipulated in these Articles; whether he has not demanded the same from us, and why it has hitherto been refused him?

"Query II. These articles, setting forth in the most expressing terms, in what manner Great Britain and Sweden ought to assist one another, can either of these two Allies take upon him to prescribe to the other who requires his assistance a way of lending him it not expressed in the treaty; and if that other Ally does not think it for his interest to accept of the same, but still insists upon the performance of the treaty, can he from thence take a pretence, not only to withhold the stipulated assistance, but also to use his Ally in a hostile way, and to join with his enemies against him? If this is not justifiable, as even common sense tells us it is not, how can the reason stand good, which we allege amongst others, for using the King of Sweden as we do, id est, that demanding a literal performance of his alliance with us, he would not accept the treaty of neutrality for his German provinces, which we proposed to him some years ago, a treaty which, not to mention its partiality in favour of the enemies of Sweden, and that it was calculated only for our own interest, and for to prevent all disturbance in the empire, whilst we were engaged in a war against France, the King of Sweden had so much less reason to rely upon, as he was to conclude it with those very enemies, that had every one of them broken several treaties in beginning the present war against him, and as it was to be guaranteed by those powers, who were also every one of them guarantees of the broken treaties, without having performed their guarantee?

"Query III. How can we make the words in the 7th Article, that in assisting our injured Ally we shall not desist before he shall be satisfied in all things, agree with our endeavouring, to the contrary, to help the enemies of that Prince, though all unjust aggressors, not only to take one province after the other from him, but also to remain undisturbed possessors thereof, blaming all along the King of Sweden for not tamely submitting thereunto?

"Query IV. The treaty concluded in the year 1661, between Great Britain and Sweden, being in the 11th Article confirmed, and the said treaty forbidding expressly one of the confederates either himself or his subjects to lend or to sell to the other's enemies, men-of-war or ships of defence; the 13th Article of this present treaty forbidding also expressly the subjects of either of the Allies to help anyways the enemies of the other, to the inconvenience and loss of such an Ally; should we not have accused the Swedes of the most notorious breach of this treaty, had they, during our late war with the French, lent them their own fleet, the better to execute any design of theirs against us, or had they, notwithstanding our representations to the contrary, suffered their subjects to furnish the French with ships of 50, 60, and 70 guns! Now, if we turn the tables, and remember upon how many occasions our fleet has of late been entirely subservient to the designs of the enemies of Sweden, even in most critical times, and that the Czar of Muscovy has actually above a dozen English-built ships in his fleet, will it not be very difficult for us to excuse in ourselves what we should most certainly have blamed, if done by others?

"Article XVII. The obligation shall not be so far extended as that all friendship and mutual commerce with the enemies of that Ally (that requires the help) shall be taken away; for supposing that one of the confederates should send his auxiliaries, and should not be engaged in the war himself, it shall then be lawful for the subjects to trade and commerce with that enemy of that Ally that is engaged in the war, also directly and safely to merchandise with such enemies, for all goods not expressly forbid and called contraband, as in a special treaty of commerce hereafter shall be appointed.

"Query I. This Article being the only one out of twenty-two whose performance we have now occasion to insist upon from the Swedes, the question will be whether we ourselves, in regard to Sweden, have performed all the other articles as it was our part to do, and whether in demanding of the King of Sweden the executing of this Article, we have promised that we would also do our duty as to all the rest; if not, may not the Swedes say that we complain unjustly of the breach of one single Article, when we ourselves may perhaps be found guilty of having in the most material points either not executed or even acted against the whole treaty?

"Query II. Whether the liberty of commerce one Ally is, by virtue of this Article, to enjoy with the other's enemies, ought to have no limitation at all, neither as to time nor place; in short, whether it ought even to be extended so far as to destroy the very end of this Treaty, which is the promoting the safety and security of one another's kingdoms?

"Query III. Whether in case the French had in the late wars made themselves masters of Ireland or Scotland, and either in new-made seaports, or the old ones, endeavoured by trade still more firmly to establish themselves in their new conquest, we, in such a case, should have thought the Swedes our true allies and friends, had they insisted upon this Article to trade with the French in the said seaports taken from us, and to furnish them there with several necessaries of war, nay, even with armed ships, whereby the French might the easier have annoyed us here in England?

"Query IV. Whether, if we had gone about to hinder a trade so prejudicial to us, and in order thereunto brought up all Swedish ships going to the said seaports, we should not highly have exclaimed against the Swedes, had they taken from thence a pretence to join their fleet with the French, to occasion the losing of any of our dominions, and even to encourage the invasion upon us, have their fleet at hand to promote the same?

"Query V. Whether upon an impartial examination this would not have been a case exactly parallel to that we insist upon, as to a free Trade to the seaports the Czar has taken from Sweden, and to our present behaviour, upon the King of Sweden's hindering the same?

"Query VI. Whether we have not ever since Oliver Cromwell's time till 1710, in all our wars with France and Holland, without any urgent necessity at all, brought up and confiscated Swedish ships, though not going to any prohibited ports, and that to a far greater number and value, than all those the Swedes have now taken from us, and whether the Swedes have ever taken a pretence from thence to join with our enemies, and to send whole squadrons of ships to their assistance?

"Query VII. Whether, if we inquire narrowly into the state of commerce, as it has been carried on for these many years, we shall not find that the trade of the above-mentioned places was not so very necessary to us, at least not so far as to be put into the balance with the preservation of a Protestant confederate nation, much less to give us a just reason to make war against that nation, which, though not declared, has done it more harm than the united efforts of all its enemies?

"Query VIII. Whether, if it happened two years ago, that this trade became something more necessary to us than formerly, it is not easily proved, that it was occasioned only by the Czar's forcing us out of our old channel of trade to Archangel, and bringing us to Petersburg, and our complying therewith. So that all the inconveniences we laboured under upon that account ought to have been laid to the Czar's door, and not to the King of Sweden's?

"Query IX. Whether the Czar did not in the very beginning of 1715 again permit us to trade our old way to Archangel, and whether our Ministers had not notice thereof a great while before our fleet was sent that year to protect our trade to Petersburg, which by this alteration in the Czar's resolution was become as unnecessary for us as before?

"Query X. Whether the King of Sweden had not declared, that if we would forbear trading to Petersburg, etc., which he looked upon as ruinous to his kingdom, he would in no manner disturb our trade, neither in the Baltic nor anywhere else; but that in case we would not give him this slight proof of our friendship, he should be excused if the innocent came to suffer with the guilty?

"Query XI. Whether, by our insisting upon the trade to the ports prohibited by the King of Sweden, which besides it being unnecessary to us, hardly makes one part in ten of that we carry on in the Baltic, we have not drawn upon us the hazards that our trade has run all this while, been ourselves the occasion of our great expenses in fitting out fleets for its protection, and by our joining with the enemies of Sweden, fully justified his Swedish Majesty's resentment; had it ever gone so far as to seize and confiscate without distinction all our ships and effects, wheresoever he found them, either within or without his kingdoms?

"Query XII. If we were so tender of our trade to the northern ports in general, ought we not in policy rather to have considered the hazard that trade runs by the approaching ruin of Sweden, and by the Czar's becoming the whole and sole master of the Baltic, and all the naval stores we want from thence? Have we not also suffered greater hardships and losses in the said trade from the Czar, than that amounting only to sixty odd thousand pounds (whereof, by the way, two parts in three may perhaps be disputable), which provoked us first to send twenty men-of-war in the Baltic with order to attack the Swedes wherever they met them? And yet, did not this very Czar, this very aspiring and dangerous prince, last summer command the whole confederate fleet, as it was called, of which our men-of-war made the most considerable part? The first instance that ever was of a Foreign Potentate having the command given him of the English fleet, the bulwark of our nation; and did not our said men-of-war afterwards convey his (the Czar's) transport ships and troops on board of them, in their return from Zealand, protecting them from the Swedish fleet, which else would have made a considerable havoc amongst them?

"Query XIII. Suppose now, we had, on the contrary, taken hold of the great and many complaints our merchants have made of the ill-usage they meet from the Czar, to have sent our fleet to show our resentment against that prince, to prevent his great and pernicious designs even to us, to assist Sweden pursuant to this Treaty, and effectually to restore the peace in the North, would not that have been more for our interest, more necessary, more honourable and just, and more according to our Treaty; and would not the several 100,000 pounds these our Northern expeditions have cost the nation, have been thus better employed?

"Query XIV. If the preserving and securing our trade against the Swedes has been the only and real object of all our measures, as to the Northern affairs, how came we the year before the last to leave eight men-of-war in the Baltic and at Copenhagen, when we had no more trade there to protect, and how came Admiral Norris last summer, although he and the Dutch together made up the number of twenty-six men-of-war, and consequently were too strong for the Swedes, to attempt anything against our trade under their convoy; yet to lay above two whole months of the best season in the Sound, without convoying our and the Dutch merchantmen to the several ports they were bound for, whereby they were kept in the Baltic so late that their return could not but be very hazardous, as it even proved, both to them and our men-of-war themselves? Will not the world be apt to think that the hopes of forcing the King of Sweden to an inglorious and disadvantageous peace, by which the Duchies of Bremen and Verden ought to be added to the Hanover dominions, or that some other such view, foreign, if not contrary, to the true and old interest of Great Britain, had then a greater influence upon all these our proceedings than the pretended care of our trade?

"Article XVIII. For as much as it seems convenient for the preservation of the liberty of navigation and commerce in the Baltic Sea, that a firm and exact friendship should be kept between the Kings of Sweden and Denmark; and whereas the former Kings of Sweden and Denmark did oblige themselves mutually, not only by the public Articles of Peace made in the camp of Copenhagen, on the 27th of May, 1660, and by the ratifications of the agreement interchanged on both sides, sacredly and inviolably to observe all and every one of the clauses comprehended in the said agreement, but also declared together to ... Charles II., King of Great Britain ... a little before the treaty concluded between England and Sweden in the year 1665, that they would stand sincerely ... to all ... of the Articles of the said peace ... whereupon Charles II., with the approbation and consent of both the forementioned Kings of Sweden and Denmark, took upon himself a little after the Treaty concluded between England and Sweden, 1st March, 1665, to wit 9th October, 1665, guarantee of the same agreements.... Whereas an instrument of peace between ... the Kings of Sweden and Denmark happened to be soon after these concluded at Lunden in Schonen, in 1679, which contains an express transaction, and repetition and confirmation of the Treaties concluded at Roskild, Copenhagen, and Westphalia; therefore ... the King of Great Britain binds himself by the force of this Treaty ... that if either of the Kings of Sweden and Denmark shall consent to the violation, either of all the agreements, or of one or more articles comprehended in them, and consequently if either of the Kings shall to the prejudice of the person, provinces, territories, islands, goods, dominions and rights of the other, which by the force of the agreements so often repeated, and made in the camp of Copenhagen, on the 27th of May, 1660, as also of those made in the ... peace at Lunden in Schonen in 1679, were attributed to every one that was interested and comprehended in the words of the peace, should either by himself or by others, presume, or secretly design or attempt, or by open molestations, or by any injury, or by any violence of arms, attempt anything; that then the ... King of Great Britain ... shall first of all, by his interposition, perform all the offices of a friend and princely ally, which may serve towards the keeping inviolable all the frequently mentioned agreements, and of every article comprehended in them, and consequently towards the preservation of peace between both kings; that afterwards if the King, who is the beginner of such prejudice, or any molestation or injury, contrary to all agreements, and contrary to any articles comprehended in them, shall refuse after being admonished ... then the King of Great Britain ... shall ... assist him that is injured as by the present agreements between the Kings of Great Britain and Sweden in such cases is determined and agreed.

"Query. Does not this article expressly tell us how to remedy the disturbances our trade in the Baltic might suffer, in case of a misunderstanding betwixt the Kings of Sweden and Denmark, by obliging both these Princes to keep all the Treaties of Peace that have been concluded between them from 1660-1670, and in case either of them should in an hostile manner act against the said Treaties, by assisting the other against the aggressor? How comes it then that we don't make use of so just a remedy against an evil we are so great sufferers by? Can anybody, though ever so partial, deny but the King of Denmark, though seemingly a sincere friend to the King of Sweden, from the peace of Travendahl till he went out of Saxony against the Muscovites, fell very unjustly upon him immediately after, taking ungenerously advantage of the fatal battle of Pultava? Is not then the King of Denmark the violator of all the above-mentioned Treaties, and consequently the true author of the disturbances our trade meets with in the Baltic? Why in God's name don't we, according to this article, assist Sweden against him, and why do we, on the contrary, declare openly against the injured King of Sweden, send hectoring and threatening memorials to him, upon the least advantage he has over his enemies, as we did last summer upon his entering Norway, and even order our fleets to act openly against him in conjunction with the Danes?

"Article XIX. There shall be 'stricter confederacy and union between the above-mentioned Kings of Great Britain and Sweden, for the future, for the defence and preservation of the Protestant, Evangelic, and reformed religion.'

"Query I. How do we, according to this article, join with Sweden to assert, protect, and preserve the Protestant religion? Don't we suffer that nation, which has always been a bulwark to the said religion, most unmercifully to be torn to pieces?... Don't we ourselves give a helping hand towards its destruction? And why all this? Because our merchants have lost their ships to the value of sixty odd thousand pounds. For this loss, and nothing else, was the pretended reason why, in the year 1715, we sent our fleet in the Baltic, at the expense of £200,000; and as to what our merchants have suffered since, suppose we attribute it to our threatening memorials as well as open hostilities against the King of Sweden, must we not even then own that that Prince's resentment has been very moderate?

"Query II. How can other Princes, and especially our fellow Protestants, think us sincere in what we have made them believe as to our zeal in spending millions of lives and money for to secure the Protestant interest only in one single branch of it, I mean the Protestant succession here, when they see that that succession has hardly taken place, before we, only for sixty odd thousand pounds, (for let us always remember that this paltry sum was the first pretence for our quarrelling with Sweden) go about to undermine the very foundation of that interest in general, by helping, as we do, entirely to sacrifice Sweden, the old and sincere protector of the Protestants, to its neighbours, of which some are professed Papists, some worse, and some, at least, but lukewarm Protestants?

"Article XX. Therefore, that a reciprocal faith of the Allies and their perseverance in this agreement may appear ... both the fore-mentioned kings mutually oblige themselves, and declare that ... they will not depart a tittle from the genuine and common sense of all and every article of this treaty under any pretences of friendship, profit, former treaty, agreement, and promise, or upon any colour whatsoever: but that they will most fully and readily, either by themselves, or ministers, or subjects, put in execution whatsoever they have promised in this treaty ... without any hesitation, exception, or excuse....

"Query I. Inasmuch as this article sets forth that, at the time of concluding of the treaty, we were under no engagement contrary to it, and that it were highly unjust should we afterwards, and while this treaty is in force, which is eighteen years after the day it was signed, have entered into any such engagements, how can we justify to the world our late proceedings against the King of Sweden, which naturally seem the consequences of a treaty either of our own making with the enemies of that Prince, or of some Court or other that at present influences our measures?

"Query II. The words in this article ... how in the name of honour, faith, and justice, do they agree with the little and pitiful pretences we now make use of, not only for not assisting Sweden, pursuant to this treaty, but even for going about so heartily as we do to destroy it?

"Article XXI. This defensive treaty shall last for eighteen years, before the end of which the confederate kings may ... again treat.

"Ratification of the abovesaid treaty. We, having seen and considered this treaty, have approved and confirmed the same in all and every particular article and clause as by the present. We do approve the same for us, our heirs, and successors; assuring and promising our princely word that we shall perform and observe sincerely and in good earnest all those things that are therein contained, for the better confirmation whereof we have ordered our great seal of England to be put to these presents, which were given at our palace of Kensington, 25th of February, in the year of our Lord 1700, and in the 11th year of our reign (Gulielmus Rex).[22]

"Query. How can any of us that declares himself for the late happy revolution, and that is a true and grateful lover of King William's for ever-glorious memory ... yet bear with the least patience, that the said treaty should (that I may again use the words of the 20th article) be departed from, under any pretence of profit, or upon any colour whatsoever, especially so insignificant and trifling a one as that which has been made use of for two years together to employ our ships, our men, and our money, to accomplish the ruin of Sweden, that same Sweden whose defence and preservation this great and wise monarch of ours has so solemnly promised, and which he always looked upon to be of the utmost necessity for to secure the Protestant interest in Europe?"

FOOTNOTE:

[22] The treaty was concluded at the Hague on the 6th and 16th January, 1700, and ratified by William III. on February 5th, 1700.

CHAPTER V

Before entering upon an analysis of the pamphlet headed, "Truth is but truth, as it is timed," with which we shall conclude the Introduction to the Diplomatic Revelations, some preliminary remarks on the general history of Russian politics appear opportune.

The overwhelming influence of Russia has taken Europe at different epochs by surprise, startled the peoples of the West, and been submitted to as a fatality, or resisted only by convulsions. But alongside the fascination exercised by Russia, there runs an ever-reviving scepticism, dogging her like a shadow, growing with her growth, mingling shrill notes of irony with the cries of agonising peoples, and mocking her very grandeur as a histrionic attitude taken up to dazzle and to cheat. Other empires have met with similar doubts in their infancy; Russia has become a colossus without outliving them. She affords the only instance in history of an immense empire, the very existence of whose power, even after world-wide achievements, has never ceased to be treated like a matter of faith rather than like a matter of fact. From the outset of the eighteenth century to our days, no author, whether he intended to exalt or to check Russia, thought it possible to dispense with first proving her existence.

But whether we be spiritualists or materialists with respect to Russia—whether we consider her power as a palpable fact, or as the mere vision of the guilt-stricken consciences of the European peoples—the question remains the same: "How did this power, or this phantom of a power, contrive to assume such dimensions as to rouse on the one side the passionate assertion, and on the other the angry denial of its threatening the world with a rehearsal of Universal Monarchy?" At the beginning of the eighteenth century Russia was regarded as a mushroom creation extemporised by the genius of Peter the Great. Schloezer thought it a discovery to have found out that she possessed a past; and in modern times, writers, like Fallmerayer, unconsciously following in the track beaten by Russian historians, have deliberately asserted that the northern spectre which frightens the Europe of the nineteenth century already overshadowed the Europe of the ninth century. With them the policy of Russia begins with the first Ruriks, and has, with some interruptions indeed, been systematically continued to the present hour.

Ancient maps of Russia are unfolded before us, displaying even larger European dimensions than she can boast of now: her perpetual movement of aggrandizement from the ninth to the eleventh century is anxiously pointed out; we are shown Oleg launching 88,000 men against Byzantium, fixing his shield as a trophy on the gate of that capital, and dictating an ignominious treaty to the Lower Empire; Igor making it tributary; Sviataslaff glorying, "the Greeks supply me with gold, costly stuffs, rice, fruits and wine; Hungary furnishes cattle and horses; from Russia I draw honey, wax, furs, and men"; Vladimir conquering the Crimea and Livonia, extorting a daughter from the Greek Emperor, as Napoleon did from the German Emperor, blending the military sway of a northern conqueror with the theocratic despotism of the Porphyro-geniti, and becoming at once the master of his subjects on earth, and their protector in heaven.

Yet, in spite of the plausible parallelism suggested by these reminiscences, the policy of the first Ruriks differs fundamentally from that of modern Russia. It was nothing more nor less than the policy of the German barbarians inundating Europe—the history of the modern nations beginning only after the deluge has passed away. The Gothic period of Russia in particular forms but a chapter of the Norman conquests. As the empire of Charlemagne precedes the foundation of modern France, Germany, and Italy, so the empire of the Ruriks precedes the foundation of Poland, Lithuania, the Baltic Settlements, Turkey, and Muscovy itself. The rapid movement of aggrandizement was not the result of deep-laid schemes, but the natural offspring of the primitive organization of Norman conquest—vassalship without fiefs, or fiefs consisting only in tributes—the necessity of fresh conquests being kept alive by the uninterrupted influx of new Varangian adventurers, panting for glory and plunder. The chiefs, becoming anxious for repose, were compelled by the Faithful Band to move on, and in Russian, as in French Normandy, there arrived the moment when the chiefs despatched on new predatory excursions their uncontrollable and insatiable companions-in-arms with the single view to get rid of them. Warfare and organization of conquest on the part of the first Ruriks differ in no point from those of the Normans in the rest of Europe. If Slavonian tribes were subjected not only by the sword, but also by mutual convention, this singularity is due to the exceptional position of those tribes, placed between a northern and eastern invasion, and embracing the former as a protection from the latter. The same magic charm which attracted other northern barbarians to the Rome of the West attracted the Varangians to the Rome of the East. The very migration of the Russian capital—Rurik fixing it at Novgorod, Oleg removing it to Kiev, and Sviataslaff attempting to establish it in Bulgaria— proves beyond doubt that the invader was only feeling his way, and considered Russia as a mere halting-place from which to wander on in search of an empire in the South. If modern Russia covets the possession of Constantinople to establish her dominion over the world, the Ruriks were, on the contrary, forced by the resistance of Byzantium, under Zimiskes, definitively to establish their dominion in Russia.

It may be objected that victors and vanquished amalgamated more quickly in Russia than in any other conquest of the northern barbarians, that the chiefs soon commingled themselves with the Slavonians—as shown by their marriages and their names. But then, it should be recollected that the Faithful Band, which formed at once their guard and their privy council, remained exclusively composed of Varangians; that Vladimir, who marks the summit, and Yaroslav, who marks the commencing decline of Gothic Russia, were seated on her throne by the arms of the Varangians. If any Slavonian influence is to be acknowledged in this epoch, it is that of Novgorod, a Slavonian State, the traditions, policy, and tendencies of which were so antagonistic to those of modern Russia that the one could found her existence only on the ruins of the other. Under Yaroslav the supremacy of the Varangians is broken, but simultaneously with it disappears the conquering tendency of the first period, and the decline of Gothic Russia begins. The history of that decline, more still than that of the conquest and formation, proves the exclusively Gothic character of the Empire of the Ruriks.

The incongruous, unwieldy, and precocious Empire heaped together by the Ruriks, like the other empires of similar growth, is broken up into appanages, divided and subdivided among the descendants of the conquerors, dilacerated by feudal wars, rent to pieces by the intervention of foreign peoples. The paramount authority of the Grand Prince vanishes before the rival claims of seventy princes of the blood. The attempt of Andrew of Susdal at recomposing some large limbs of the empire by the removal of the capital from Kiev to Vladimir proves successful only in propagating the decomposition from the South to the centre. Andrew's third successor resigns even the last shadow of supremacy, the title of Grand Prince, and the merely nominal homage still offered him. The appanages to the South and to the West become by turns Lithuanian, Polish, Hungarian, Livonian, Swedish. Kiev itself, the ancient capital, follows destinies of its own, after having dwindled down from a seat of the Grand Princedom to the territory of a city. Thus, the Russia of the Normans completely disappears from the stage, and the few weak reminiscences in which it still outlived itself, dissolve before the terrible apparition of Genghis Khan. The bloody mire of Mongolian slavery, not the rude glory of the Norman epoch, forms the cradle of Muscovy, and modern Russia is but a metamorphosis of Muscovy.

The Tartar yoke lasted from 1237 to 1462—more than two centuries; a yoke not only crushing, but dishonouring and withering the very soul of the people that fell its prey. The Mongol Tartars established a rule of systematic terror, devastation and wholesale massacre forming its institutions. Their numbers being scanty in proportion to their enormous conquests, they wanted to magnify them by a halo of consternation, and to thin, by wholesale slaughter, the populations which might rise in their rear. In their creations of desert they were, besides, led by the same economical principle which has depopulated the Highlands of Scotland and the Campagna di Roma—the conversion of men into sheep, and of fertile lands and populous abodes into pasturage.

The Tartar yoke had already lasted a hundred years before Muscovy emerged from its obscurity. To entertain discord among the Russian princes, and secure their servile submission, the Mongols had restored the dignity of the Grand Princedom. The strife among the Russian princes for this dignity was, as a modern author has it, "an abject strife—the strife of slaves, whose chief weapon was calumny, and who were always ready to denounce each other to their cruel rulers; wrangling for a degraded throne, whence they could not move but with plundering, parricidal hands—hands filled with gold and stained with gore; which they dared not ascend without grovelling, nor retain but on their knees, prostrate and trembling beneath the scimitar of a Tartar, always ready to roll under his feet those servile crowns, and the heads by which they were worn." It was in this infamous strife that the Moscow branch won at last the race. In 1328 the crown of the Grand Princedom, wrested from the branch of Tver by dint of denunciation and assassination, was picked up at the feet of Usbeck Khan by Yury, the elder brother of Ivan Kalita. Ivan I. Kalita, and Ivan III., surnamed the Great, personate Muscovy rising by means of the Tartar yoke, and Muscovy getting an independent power by the disappearance of the Tartar rule. The whole policy of Muscovy, from its first entrance into the historical arena, is resumed in the history of these two individuals.

The policy of Ivan Kalita was simply this: to play the abject tool of the Khan, thus to borrow his power, and then to turn it round upon his princely rivals and his own subjects. To attain this end, he had to insinuate himself with the Tartars by dint of cynical adulation, by frequent journeys to the Golden Horde, by humble prayers for the hand of Mongol princesses, by a display of unbounded zeal for the Khan's interest, by the unscrupulous execution of his orders, by atrocious calumnies against his own kinsfolk, by blending in himself the characters of the Tartar's hangman, sycophant, and slave-in-chief. He perplexed the Khan by continuous revelations of secret plots. Whenever the branch of Tver betrayed a velleité of national independence, he hurried to the Horde to denounce it. Wherever he met with resistance, he introduced the Tartar to trample it down. But it was not sufficient to act a character; to make it acceptable, gold was required. Perpetual bribery of the Khan and his grandees was the only sure foundation upon which to raise his fabric of deception and usurpation. But how was the slave to get the money wherewith to bribe the master? He persuaded the Khan to instal him his tax-gatherer throughout all the Russian appanages. Once invested with this function, he extorted money under false pretences. The wealth accumulated by the dread held out of the Tartar name, he used to corrupt the Tartars themselves. By a bribe he induced the primate to transfer his episcopal seat from Vladimir to Moscow, thus making the latter the capital of the empire, because the religious capital, and coupling the power of the Church with that of his throne. By a bribe he allured the Boyards of the rival princes into treason against their chiefs, and attracted them to himself as their centre. By the joint influence of the Mahometan Tartar, the Greek Church, and the Boyards, he unites the princes holding appanages into a crusade against the most dangerous of them—the prince of Tver; and then having driven his recent allies by bold attempts at usurpation into resistance against himself, into a war for the public good, he draws not the sword but hurries to the Khan. By bribes and delusion again, he seduces him into assassinating his kindred rivals under the most cruel torments. It was the traditional policy of the Tartar to check the Russian princes the one by the other, to feed their dissensions, to cause their forces to equiponderate, and to allow none to consolidate himself. Ivan Kalita converts the Khan into the tool by which he rids himself of his most dangerous competitors, and weighs down every obstacle to his own usurping march. He does not conquer the appanages, but surreptitiously turns the rights of the Tartar conquest to his exclusive profit. He secures the succession of his son through the same means by which he had raised the Grand Princedom of Muscovy, that strange compound of princedom and serfdom. During his whole reign he swerves not once from the line of policy he had traced to himself; clinging to it with a tenacious firmness, and executing it with methodical boldness. Thus he becomes the founder of the Muscovite power, and characteristically his people call him Kalita—that is, the purse, because it was the purse and not the sword with which he cut his way. The very period of his reign witnesses the sudden growth of the Lithuanian power which dismembers the Russian appanages from the West, while the Tartar squeezes them into one mass from the East. Ivan, while he dared not repulse the one disgrace, seemed anxious to exaggerate the other. He was not to be seduced from following up his ends by the allurements of glory, the pangs of conscience, or the lassitude of humiliation. His whole system may be expressed in a few words: the machiavelism of the usurping slave. His own weakness—his slavery—he turned into the mainspring of his strength.

The policy traced by Ivan I. Kalita is that of his successors; they had only to enlarge the circle of its application. They followed it up laboriously, gradually, inflexibly. From Ivan I. Kalita, we may, therefore, pass at once to Ivan III., surnamed the Great.

At the commencement of his reign (1462-1505) Ivan III. was still a tributary to the Tartars; his authority was still contested by the princes holding appanages; Novgorod, the head of the Russian republics, reigned over the north of Russia; Poland-Lithuania was striving for the conquest of Muscovy; lastly, the Livonian knights were not yet disarmed. At the end of his reign we behold Ivan III. seated on an independent throne, at his side the daughter of the last emperor of Byzantium, at his feet Kasan, and the remnant of the Golden Horde flocking to his court; Novgorod and the other Russian republics enslaved—Lithuania diminished, and its king a tool in Ivan's hands—the Livonian knights vanquished. Astonished Europe, at the commencement of Ivan's reign, hardly aware of the existence of Muscovy, hemmed in between the Tartar and the Lithuanian, was dazzled by the sudden appearance of an immense empire on its eastern confines, and Sultan Bajazet himself, before whom Europe trembled, heard for the first time the haughty language of the Muscovite. How, then, did Ivan accomplish these high deeds? Was he a hero? The Russian historians themselves show him up a confessed coward.

Let us shortly survey his principal contests, in the sequence in which he undertook and concluded them—his contests with the Tartars, with Novgorod, with the princes holding appanages, and lastly with Lithuania-Poland.

Ivan rescued Muscovy from the Tartar yoke, not by one bold stroke, but by the patient labour of about twenty years. He did not break the yoke, but disengaged himself by stealth. Its overthrow, accordingly, has more the look of the work of nature than the deed of man. When the Tartar monster expired at last, Ivan appeared at its deathbed like a physician, who prognosticated and speculated on death rather than like a warrior who imparted it. The character of every people enlarges with its enfranchisement from a foreign yoke; that of Muscovy in the hands of Ivan seems to diminish. Compare only Spain in its struggles against the Arabs with Muscovy in its struggles against the Tartars.

At the period of Ivan's accession to the throne, the Golden Horde had long since been weakened, internally by fierce feuds, externally by the separation from them of the Nogay Tartars, the eruption of Timour Tamerlane, the rise of the Cossacks, and the hostility of the Crimean Tartars. Muscovy, on the contrary, by steadily pursuing the policy traced by Ivan Kalita, had grown to a mighty mass, crushed, but at the same time compactly united by the Tartar chain. The Khans, as if struck by a charm, had continued to remain instruments of Muscovite aggrandizement and concentration. By calculation they had added to the power of the Greek Church, which, in the hand of the Muscovite grand princes, proved the deadliest weapon against them.

In rising against the Horde, the Muscovite had not to invent but only to imitate the Tartars themselves. But Ivan did not rise. He humbly acknowledged himself a slave of the Golden Horde. By bribing a Tartar woman he seduced the Khan into commanding the withdrawal from Muscovy of the Mongol residents. By similar and imperceptible and surreptitious steps he duped the Khan into successive concessions, all ruinous to his sway. He thus did not conquer, but filch strength. He does not drive, but manœuvre his enemy out of his strongholds. Still continuing to prostrate himself before the Khan's envoys, and to proclaim himself his tributary, he eludes the payment of the tribute under false pretences, employing all the stratagems of a fugitive slave who dare not front his owner, but only steal out of his reach. At last the Mongol awakes from his torpor, and the hour of battle sounds. Ivan, trembling at the mere semblance of an armed encounter, attempts to hide himself behind his own fear, and to disarm the fury of his enemy by withdrawing the object upon which to wreak his vengeance. He is only saved by the intervention of the Crimean Tartars, his allies. Against a second invasion of the Horde, he ostentatiously gathers together such disproportionate forces that the mere rumour of their number parries the attack. At the third invasion, from the midst of 200,000 men, he absconds a disgraced deserter. Reluctantly dragged back, he attempts to haggle for conditions of slavery, and at last, pouring into his army his own servile fear, he involves it in a general and disorderly flight. Muscovy was then anxiously awaiting its irretrievable doom, when it suddenly hears that by an attack on their capital made by the Crimean Khan, the Golden Horde has been forced to withdraw, and has, on its retreat, been destroyed by the Cossacks and Nogay Tartars. Thus defeat was turned into success, and Ivan had overthrown the Golden Horde, not by fighting it himself, but by challenging it through a feigned desire of combat into offensive movements, which exhausted its remnants of vitality and exposed it to the fatal blows of the tribes of its own race whom he had managed to turn into his allies. He caught one Tartar with another Tartar. As the immense danger he had himself summoned proved unable to betray him into one single trait of manhood, so his miraculous triumph did not infatuate him even for one moment. With cautious circumspection he dared not incorporate Kasan with Muscovy, but made it over to sovereigns belonging to the family of Menghi-Ghirei, his Crimean ally, to hold it, as it were, in trust for Muscovy. With the spoils of the vanquished Tartar, he enchained the victorious Tartar. But if too prudent to assume, with the eye-witnesses of his disgrace, the airs of a conqueror, this impostor did fully understand how the downfall of the Tartar empire must dazzle at a distance—with what halo of glory it would encircle him, and how it would facilitate a magnificent entry among the European Powers. Accordingly he assumed abroad the theatrical attitude of the conqueror, and, indeed, succeeded in hiding under a mask of proud susceptibility and irritable haughtiness the obtrusiveness of the Mongol serf, who still remembered kissing the stirrup of the Khan's meanest envoy. He aped in more subdued tone the voice of his old masters, which terrified his soul. Some standing phrases of modern

Russian diplomacy, such as the magnanimity, the wounded dignity of the master, are borrowed from the diplomatic instructions of Ivan III.

After the surrender of Kasan, he set out on a long-planned expedition against Novgorod, the head of the Russian republics. If the overthrow of the Tartar yoke was, in his eyes, the first condition of Muscovite greatness, the overthrow of Russian freedom was the second. As the republic of Viatka had declared itself neutral between Muscovy and the Horde, and the republic of Tskof, with its twelve cities, had shown symptoms of disaffection, Ivan flattered the latter and affected to forget the former, meanwhile concentrating all his forces against Novgorod the Great, with the doom of which he knew the fate of the rest of the Russian republics to be sealed. By the prospect of sharing in this rich booty, he drew after him the princes holding appanages, while he inveigled the boyards by working upon their blind hatred of Novgorodian democracy. Thus he contrived to march three armies upon Novgorod and to overwhelm it by disproportionate force. But then, in order not to keep his word to the princes, not to forfeit his immutable "Vos non vobis," at the same time apprehensive, lest Novgorod should not yet have become digestible from the want of preparatory treatment, he thought fit to exhibit a sudden moderation; to content himself with a ransom and the acknowledgment of his suzerainty; but into the act of submission of the republic he smuggled some ambiguous words which made him its supreme judge and legislator. Then he fomented the dissensions between the patricians and plebeians raging as well in Novgorod as at Florence. Of some complaints of the plebeians he took occasion to introduce himself again into the city, to have its nobles, whom he knew to be hostile to himself, sent to Moscow loaded with chains, and to break the ancient law of the republic that "none of its citizens should ever be tried or punished out of the limits of its own territory." From that moment he became supreme arbiter. "Never," say the annalists, "never since Rurik had such an event happened; never had the grand princes of Kiev and Vladimir seen the Novgorodians come and submit to them as their judges. Ivan alone could reduce Novgorod to that degree of humiliation." Seven years were employed by Ivan to corrupt the republic by the exercise of his judicial authority. Then, when he found its strength worn out, he thought the moment ripe for declaring himself. To doff his own mask of moderation, he wanted, on the part of Novgorod, a breach of the peace. As he had simulated calm endurance, so he simulated now a sudden burst of passion. Having bribed an envoy of the republic to address him during a public audience with the name of sovereign, he claimed, at once, all the rights of a despot— the self-annihilation of the republic.

CHAPTER VI

One feature characteristic of the Slavonic race must strike every observer. Almost everywhere it confined itself to an inland country, leaving the sea-borders to non-Slavonic tribes. Finno-Tartaric tribes held the shores of the Black Sea, Lithuanians and Fins those of the Baltic and White Sea. Wherever they touched the sea-board, as in the Adriatic and part of the Baltic, the Slavonians had soon to submit to foreign rule. The Russian people shared this common fate of the Slavonian race. Their home, at the time they first appear in history, was the country about the sources and upper course of the Volga and its tributaries, the Dnieper, Don, and Northern Dwina. Nowhere did their territory touch the sea except at the extremity of the Gulf of Finland. Nor had they before Peter the Great proved able to conquer any maritime outlet beside that of the White Sea, which, during three-fourths of the year, is itself enchained and immovable. The spot where Petersburg now stands had been for a thousand years past contested ground between Fins, Swedes, and Russians. All the remaining extent of coast from Polangen, near Memel, to Torrea, the whole coast of the Black Sea, from Akerman to Redut Kaleh, has been conquered later on. And, as if to witness the anti-maritime peculiarity of the Slavonic race, of all this line of coast, no portion of the Baltic coast has really adopted Russian nationality. Nor has the Circassian and Mingrelian east coast of the Black Sea. It is only the coast of the White Sea, as far as it was worth cultivating, some portion of the northern coast of the Black Sea, and part of the coast of the Sea of Azof, that have really been peopled with Russian inhabitants, who, however, despite the new circumstances in which they are placed, still refrain from taking to the sea, and obstinately stick to the land-lopers' traditions of their ancestors.

From the very outset, Peter the Great broke through all the traditions of the Slavonic race. "It is water that Russia wants." These words he addressed as a rebuke to Prince Cantemir are inscribed on the title-page of his life. The conquest of the Sea of Azof was aimed at in his first war with Turkey, the conquest of the Baltic in his war against Sweden, the conquest of the Black Sea in his second war against the Porte, and the conquest of the Caspian Sea in his fraudulent intervention in Persia. For a system of local encroachment, land was sufficient; for a system of universal aggression, water had become indispensable. It was but by the conversion of Muscovy from a country wholly of land into a sea-bordering empire, that the traditional limits of the Muscovite policy could be superseded and merged into that bold synthesis which, blending the encroaching method of the Mongol slave with the world-conquering tendencies of the Mongol master, forms the life-spring of modern Russian diplomacy.

It has been said that no great nation has ever existed, or been able to exist, in such an inland position as that of the original empire of Peter the Great; that none has ever submitted thus to see its coasts and the mouths of its rivers torn away from it; that Russia could no more leave the mouth of the Neva, the natural outlet for the produce of Northern Russia, in the hands of the Swedes, than the mouths of the Don, Dnieper, and Bug, and the Straits of Kertch, in the hands of nomadic and plundering Tartars; that the Baltic provinces, from their very geographical configuration, are naturally a corollary to whichever nation holds the country behind them; that, in one word, Peter, in this quarter, at least, but took hold of what was absolutely necessary for the natural development of his country. From this point of view, Peter the Great intended, by his war against Sweden, only rearing a Russian Liverpool, and endowing it with its indispensable strip of coast.

But then, one great fact is slighted over, the tour de force by which he transferred the capital of the Empire from the inland centre to the maritime extremity, the characteristic boldness with which he erected the new capital on the first strip of Baltic coast he conquered, almost within gunshot of the frontier, thus deliberately giving his dominions an eccentric centre. To transfer the throne of the Czars from Moscow to Petersburg was to place it in a position where it could not be safe, even from insult, until the whole coast from Libau to Tornea was subdued—a work not completed till 1809, by the conquest of Finland. "St. Petersburg is the window from which Russia can overlook Europe," said Algarotti. It was from the first a defiance to the Europeans, an incentive to further conquest to the Russians. The fortifications in our own days of Russian Poland are only a further step in the execution of the same idea. Modlin, Warsaw, Ivangorod, are more than citadels to keep a rebellious country in check. They are the same menace to the west which Petersburg, in its immediate bearing, was a hundred years ago to the north. They are to transform Russia into Panslavonia, as the Baltic provinces were to transform Muscovy into Russia.

Petersburg, the eccentric centre of the empire, pointed at once to a periphery still to be drawn.

It is, then, not the mere conquest of the Baltic provinces which separates the policy of Peter the Great from that of his ancestors, but it is the transfer of the capital which reveals the true meaning of his Baltic conquests. Petersburg was not like Muscovy, the centre of a race, but the seat of a government; not the slow work of a people, but the instantaneous creation of a man; not the medium from which the peculiarities of an inland people radiate, but the maritime extremity where they are lost; not the traditionary nucleus of a national development, but the deliberately chosen abode of a cosmopolitan intrigue. By the transfer of the capital, Peter cut off the natural ligaments which bound up the encroaching system of the old Muscovite Czars with the natural abilities and aspirations of the great Russian race. By planting his capital on the margin of a sea, he put to open defiance the anti-maritime instincts of that race, and degraded it to a mere weight in his political mechanism. Since the 16th century Muscovy had made no important acquisitions but on the side of Siberia, and to the 16th century the dubious conquests made towards the west and the south were only brought about by direct agency on the east. By the transfer of the capital, Peter proclaimed that he, on the contrary, intended working on the east and the immediately neighbouring countries through the agency of the west. If the agency through the east was narrowly circumscribed by the stationary character and the limited relations of Asiatic peoples, the agency through the west became at once illimited and universal from the movable character and the all-sided relations of Western Europe. The transfer of the capital denoted this intended change of agency, which the conquest of the Baltic provinces afforded the means of achieving, by securing at once to Russia the supremacy among the neighbouring Northern States; by putting it into immediate and constant contact with all points of Europe; by laying the basis of a material bond with the maritime Powers, which by this conquest became dependent on Russia for their naval stores; a dependence not existing as long as Muscovy, the country that produced the great bulk of the naval stores, had got no outlets of its own; while Sweden, the Power that held these outlets, had not got the country lying behind them.

If the Muscovite Czars, who worked their encroachments by the agency principally of the Tartar Khans, were obliged to tartarize Muscovy, Peter the Great, who resolved upon working through the agency of the west, was obliged to civilize Russia. In grasping upon the Baltic provinces, he seized at once the tools necessary for this process. They afforded him not only the diplomatists and the generals, the brains with which to execute his system of political and military action on the west, they yielded him, at the same time, a crop of bureaucrats, schoolmasters, and drill-sergeants, who were to drill Russians into that varnish of civilization that adapts them to the technical appliances of the Western peoples, without imbuing them with their ideas.

Neither the Sea of Azof, nor the Black Sea, nor the Caspian Sea, could open to Peter this direct passage to Europe. Besides, during his lifetime still Taganrog, Azof, the Black Sea, with its new-formed Russian fleets, ports, and dockyards, were again abandoned or given up to the Turk. The Persian conquest, too, proved a premature enterprise. Of the four wars which fill the military life of Peter the Great, his first war, that against Turkey, the fruits of which were lost in a second Turkish war, continued in one respect the traditionary struggle with the Tartars. In another respect, it was but the prelude to the war against Sweden, of which the second Turkish war forms an episode and the Persian war an epilogue. Thus the war against Sweden, lasting during twenty-one years, almost absorbs the military life of Peter the Great. Whether we consider its purpose, its results, or its endurance, we may justly call it the war of Peter the Great. His whole creation hinges upon the conquest of the Baltic coast.

Now, suppose we were altogether ignorant of the details of his operations, military and diplomatic. The mere fact that the conversion of Muscovy into Russia was brought about by its transformation from a half-Asiatic inland country into the paramount maritime Power of the Baltic, would it not enforce upon us the conclusion that England, the greatest maritime Power of that epoch—a maritime Power lying, too, at the very gates of the Baltic, where, since the middle of the 17th century, she had maintained the attitude of supreme arbiter—

that England must have had her hand in this great change, that she must have proved the main prop or the main impediment of the plans of Peter the Great, that during the long protracted and deadly struggle between Sweden and Russia she must have turned the balance, that if we do not find her straining every nerve in order to save the Swede we may be sure of her having employed all the means at her disposal for furthering the Muscovite? And yet, in what is commonly called history, England does hardly appear on the plan of this grand drama, and is represented as a spectator rather than as an actor. Real history will show that the Khans of the Golden Horde were no more instrumental in realizing the plans of Ivan III. and his predecessors than the rulers of England were in realizing the plans of Peter I. and his successors.

The pamphlets which we have reprinted, written as they were by English contemporaries of Peter the Great, are far from concurring in the common delusions of later historians. They emphatically denounce England as the mightiest tool of Russia. The same position is taken up by the pamphlet of which we shall now give a short analysis, and with which we shall conclude the introduction to the diplomatic revelations. It is entitled, "Truth is but Truth as it is timed; or, our Ministry's present measures against the Muscovite vindicated, etc., etc. Humbly dedicated to the House of C., London, 1719."

The former pamphlets we have reprinted, were written at, or shortly after, the time when, to use the words of a modern admirer of Russia, "Peter traversed the Baltic Sea as master at the head of the combined squadrons of all the northern Powers, England included, which gloried in sailing under his orders." In 1719, however, when Truth is but Truth was published, the face of affairs seemed altogether changed. Charles XII. was dead, and the English Government now pretended to side with Sweden, and to wage war against Russia. There are other circumstances connected with this anonymous pamphlet which claim particular notice. It purports to be an extract from a relation, which, on his return from Muscovy, in August, 1715, its author, by order of George I., drew up and handed over to Viscount Townshend, then Secretary of State.

"It happens," says he, "to be an advantage that at present I may own to have been the first so happy to foresee, or honest to forewarn our Court here, of the absolute necessity of our then breaking with the Czar, and shutting him out again of the Baltic." "My relation discovered his aim as to other States, and even to the German Empire, to which, although an inland Power, he had offered to annex Livonia as an Electorate, so that he could but be admitted as an elector. It drew attention to the Czar's then contemplated assumption of the title of Autocrator. Being head of the Greek Church he would be owned by the other potentates as head of the Greek Empire. I am not to say how reluctant we would be to acknowledge that title, since we have already made an ambassador treat him with the title of Imperial Majesty, which the Swede has never yet condescended to."

For some time attached to the British Embassy in Muscovy, our author, as he states, was later on "dismissed the service, because the Czar desired it," having made sure that

"I had given our Court such light into his affairs as is contained in this paper; for which I beg leave to appeal to the King, and to vouch the Viscount Townshend, who heard his Majesty give that vindication." "And yet, notwithstanding all this, I have been for these five years past kept soliciting for a very long arrear still due, and whereof I contracted the greatest part in executing a commission for her late Majesty."

The anti-Muscovite attitude, suddenly assumed by the Stanhope Cabinet, our author looks to in rather a sceptic mood.

"I do not pretend to foreclose, by this paper, the Ministry of that applause due to them from the public, when they shall satisfy us as to what the motives were which made them, till but yesterday, straiten the Swede in everything, although then our ally as much as now; or strengthen, by all the ways they could, the Czar, although under no tie, but barely that of amity with Great Britain.... At the minute I write this I learn that the gentleman who brought the Muscovites, not yet three years ago, as a royal navy, not under our protection, on their first appearance in the Baltic, is again authorized by the persons now in power, to give the Czar a second meeting in these seas. For what reason or to what good end?"

The gentleman hinted at is Admiral Norris, whose Baltic campaign against Peter I. seems, indeed, to be the original pattern upon which the recent naval campaigns of Admirals Napier and Dundas were cut out.

The restoration to Sweden of the Baltic provinces is required by the commercial as well as the political interest of Great Britain. Such is the pith of our author's argument:

"Trade is become the very life of our State; and what food is to life, naval stores are to a fleet. The whole trade we drive with all the other nations of the earth, at best, is but lucrative; this, of the north, is indispensably needful, and may not be improperly termed the sacra embole of Great Britain, as being its chiefest foreign vent, for the support of all our trade, and our safety at home. As woollen manufactures and minerals are the staple commodities of Great Britain, so are likewise naval stores those of Muscovy, as also of all those very provinces in the Baltic which the Czar has so lately wrested from the crown of Sweden. Since those provinces have been in the Czar's possession, Pernan is entirely waste. At Revel we have not one British merchant left, and all the trade which was formerly at Narwa is now brought to Petersburg.... The Swede could never possibly engross the trade of our subjects, because those seaports in his hands were but so many thoroughfares from whence these commodities were uttered, the places of their produce or manufacture lying behind those ports, in the dominions of the Czar. But, if left to the Czar, these Baltic ports are no more thoroughfares, but peculiar magazines from the inland countries of the Czar's own dominions. Having already Archangel in the White Sea, to leave him but any seaport in the Baltic were to put no less in his hands than the two keys of the general magazines of all the naval stores of Europe; it being known that Danes, Swedes, Poles, and Prussians have but single and distinct branches of those commodities in their several dominions. If the Czar should thus engross 'the supply of what we cannot do without,' where then is our fleet? Or, indeed, where is the security for all our trade to any part of the earth besides?"

If, then, the interest of British commerce requires to exclude the Czar from the Baltic, the interest of our State ought to be no less a spur to quicken us to that attempt. By the interest of our State I would be understood to mean neither the party measures of a Ministry, nor any foreign motives of a Court, but precisely what is, and ever must be, the immediate concern, either for the safety, ease, dignity, or emolument of the Crown, as well as the common weal of Great Britain. With respect to the Baltic, it has "from the earliest period of our naval power" always been considered a fundamental interest of our State: first, to prevent the rise there of any new maritime Power; and, secondly, to maintain the balance of power between Denmark and Sweden.

"One instance of the wisdom and foresight of our then truly British statesmen is the peace at Stalboa, in the year 1617. James the First was the mediator of that treaty, by which the Muscovite was obliged to give up all the provinces which he then was possessed of in the Baltic, and to be barely an inland Power on this side of Europe."

The same policy of preventing a new maritime Power from starting in the Baltic was acted upon by Sweden and Denmark.

"Who knows not that the Emperor's attempt to get a seaport in Pomerania weighed no less with the great Gustavus than any other motive for carrying his arms even into the bowels of the house of Austria? What befel, at the times of Charles Gustavus, the crown of Poland itself, who, besides it being in those days by far the mightiest of any of the northern Powers, had then a long stretch of coast on, and some ports in, the Baltic? The Danes, though then in alliance with Poland, would never allow them, even for their assistance against the Swedes, to have a fleet in the Baltic, but destroyed the Polish ships wherever they could meet them."

As to the maintenance of the balance of power between the established maritime States of the Baltic, the tradition of British policy is no less clear. "When the Swedish power gave us some uneasiness there by threatening to crush Denmark," the honour of our country was kept up by retrieving the then inequality of the balance of power.

The Commonwealth of England sent in a squadron to the Baltic which brought on the treaty of Roskild (1658), afterwards confirmed at Copenhagen (1660). The fire of straw kindled by the Danes in the times of King William III. was as speedily quenched by George Rock in the treaty of Copenhagen.

Such was the hereditary British policy.

"It never entered into the mind of the politicians of those times in order to bring the scale again to rights, to find out the happy expedient of raising a third naval Power for framing a juster balance in the Baltic.... Who has taken this counsel against Tyre, the crowning city, whose merchants are princes, whose traffickers are the honourables of the earth? Ego autem neminem nomino, quare irasci mihi nemo poterit, nisi qui ante de se noluerit confiteri. Posterity will be under some difficulty to believe that this could be the work of any of the persons now in power ... that we have opened; St. Petersburg to the Czar solely at our own expense, and without any risk to him...."

The safest line of policy would be to return to the treaty of Itolbowa, and to suffer the Muscovite no longer "to nestle in the Baltic." Yet, it may be said, that in "the present state of affairs" it would be "difficult to retrieve the advantage we have lost by not curbing, when it was more easy, the growth of the Muscovite power." A middle course may be thought more convenient.

"If we should find it consistent with the welfare of our State that the Muscovite have an inlet into the Baltic, as having, of all the princes of Europe, a country that can be made most beneficial to its prince, by uttering its produce to foreign markets. In this case, it were but reasonable to expect, on the other hand, that in return for our complying so far with his interest, for the improvement of his country, his Czarish Majesty, on his part, should demand nothing that may tend to the disturbance of another; and, therefore, contenting himself with ships of trade, should demand none of war."

"We should thus preclude his hopes of being ever more than an inland Power," but "obviate every objection of using the Czar worse than any Sovereign Prince may expect. I shall not for this give an instance of a Republic of Genoa, or another in the Baltic itself, of the Duke of Courland; but will assign Poland and Prussia, who, though both now crowned heads, have ever contented themselves with the freedom of an open traffic, without insisting on a fleet.

Or the treaty of Falczin, between the Turk and Muscovite, by which Peter was forced not only to restore Asoph, and to part with all his men-of-war in those parts, but also to content himself with the bare freedom of traffic in the Black Sea. Even an inlet in the Baltic for trade is much beyond what he could morally have promised himself not yet so long ago on the issue of his war with Sweden."

If the Czar refuse to agree to such "a healing temperament," we shall have "nothing to regret but the time we lost to exert all the means that Heaven has made us master of, to reduce him to a peace advantageous to Great Britain." War would become inevitable. In that case

"it ought no less to animate our Ministry to pursue their present measures, than fire with indignation the breast of every honest Briton that a Czar of Muscovy, who owes his naval skill to our instructions, and his grandeur to our forbearance, should so soon deny to Great Britain the terms which so few years ago he was fain to take up with from the Sublime Porte."

"'Tis every way our interest to have the Swede restored to those provinces which the Muscovite has wrested from that crown in the Baltic. Great Britain can no longer hold the balance in that sea," since she "has raised the Muscovite to be a maritime Power there.... Had we performed the articles of our alliance made by King William with the crown of Sweden, that gallant nation would ever have been a bar strong enough against the Czar coming into the Baltic.... Time must confirm us, that the Muscovite's expulsion from the Baltic is now the principal end of our Ministry."

Note from the Editor

Odin's Library Classics strives to bring you unedited and unabridged works of classical literature. As such this is the complete and unabridged version of the original English text. The English language has evolved since the writing and some of the words appear in their original form, or at least the most commonly used form at the time. This is done to protect the original intent of the author. If at any time you are unsure of the meaning of a word, please do your research on the etymology of that word. It is important to preserve the history of the English language.

Taylor Anderson

Made in the USA
Middletown, DE
31 August 2020

17735177R10031